Choose Grace

Choose Grace

Why Now is the Time

Loretta Engelhardt

BALBOA
PRESS
A DIVISION OF HAY HOUSE

Balboa Press books may be ordered through booksellers or by contacting:

Balboa Press
A Division of Hay House
1663 Liberty Drive
Bloomington, IN 47403
www.balboapress.com
1-(877) 407-4847

Because of the dynamic nature of the Internet, any web addresses or links contained in this book may have changed since publication and may no longer be valid. The views expressed in this work are solely those of the author and do not necessarily reflect the views of the publisher, and the publisher hereby disclaims any responsibility for them.

The author of this book does not dispense medical advice or prescribe the use of any technique as a form of treatment for physical, emotional, or medical problems without the advice of a physician, either directly or indirectly. The intent of the author is only to offer information of a general nature to help you in your quest for emotional and spiritual well-being. In the event you use any of the information in this book for yourself, which is your constitutional right, the author and the publisher assume no responsibility for your actions.

Any people depicted in stock imagery provided by Thinkstock are models, and such images are being used for illustrative purposes only. Certain stock imagery © Thinkstock.

Photo credits:
Cover, Jackie Klieger, jklieg@aol.com
Author Photo, Janise Witt, photographybyjanise.com.

Printed in the United States of America.

ISBN: 978-1-4525-7173-7 (sc)
ISBN: 978-1-4525-7175-1 (hc)
ISBN: 978-1-4525-7174-4 (e)
Library of Congress Control Number: 2013905915
Balboa Press rev. date: 4/30/2013

In Gratitude

For my husband, Ken, who has been a
source of pure love all these years.

TABLE OF CONTENTS

Acknowledgments

From the beginning, when I was inspired to write about grace and how it has manifested in my life, I have been supported and encouraged by important, grace-filled friends. With deep gratitude I acknowledge Carmen Gram, as she facilitated discovering the laws, states, and acts of grace within the Genesa matrix; Harvey Grady, through whom the Monitor Group speaks; my writer group friends, Cynthia Strom and Shirley Willis, who listened with love at our monthly gatherings and asked for expansion and clarity as the manuscript unfolded; and my friends Kathy Dunham and Jackie Klieger, who generously shared with me the impact the grace material had on their lives just at the time I was questioning the value of expressing this information.

Further appreciation goes to my dear friends Marlene Wilson, Julie Grady, and Jeannie Marini, who read early drafts and offered me enough encouragement to proceed with assurance. I acknowledge my high self or solar angel, whom I call Beloved, my guides and all inspiration not in physical form that I call on for wisdom and assistance. And I am grateful for you, the reader, as you have chosen to bring grace into your life.

INTRODUCTION
LEARNING ABOUT GRACE

When I was a child, my parents encouraged my brother and me to begin and end each day with an expression of dedication and an expression of gratitude. They adhered to this adage, popular in the 1940s: "The family that prays together stays together." As a six-year-old, I remember saying this morning offering each day, "I offer all my thoughts, words, and deeds in love for the good of all." Often we would say our intention aloud as we sat at the breakfast table before going our separate ways to play or to work. Although this daily offering seemed tiresome and contrived at times, I now realize this simple intention helped set into motion my grace-filled life.

At that time in my child world, I thought grace had a religious connotation associated with Christianity. I now know that grace cannot be limited to any religion, particular religious practice, or historical perspective. Since grace is order within and beyond form, it is available for all. This order or organization is of a higher order and cannot be defined as content but can be glimpsed as an experience when aligning with divinity.

As an adult, I now begin each day by thinking or saying aloud, "I offer all my thoughts, words, and actions in love for the good of all. May the golden light of grace surround me and all that I touch. May grace be present throughout the world where need and acceptance are perceived."

We may come to know that grace is already present in all aspects of our daily life, as exemplified in our working vocabulary: "amazing grace," "a grace period," "saving grace," "graceful," "graced by your presence," "grace notes," and "staying in one's good graces." What engaging imagery these phrases invoke!

From my earliest recollections of childhood, I knew my life was magic. I felt protected, powerful, and guided. At first that sense of magic was just a knowing. I accepted that I was loved and appreciated for who I was. My perception as a child was that I could do whatever I wanted and that whatever I needed was available. I had an authentic sense of abundance. At the same time, I was always aware of a desire to be moderate and kind in my actions and requests. I know now that I was in a state of grace and that much of my life is an act of grace. My intention in writing this book is to explore that knowing and to put into words those qualities of grace I have come to know more fully. I offer this story in thanksgiving for the presence of grace in my life and as an invitation to you, the reader, to explore each of your grace-filled lives.

To accomplish this intention, I have divided these life stories into chapters representing spans of time and what I came to know and experience in each time span. As you read of my life, reflect upon the expressions and acts of grace highlighted to enliven those qualities of grace in your life.

The chapters of grace in my life include:

Awakening and Adjusting—Birth to Eighteen Years of Age

Accepting Responsibility as an Adult—Ages Nineteen to Forty

Questioning and Refining—Ages Forty-One to Sixty

Sharing and Releasing—Age Sixty-One and Onward

Many tools are available to stay healthy, evolve, and transcend in this outstanding time of change and seeming chaos. One of the most powerful tools to enhance our personal health and evolve spiritually is grace. We begin to be aware of grace by exploring our own life experiences and perhaps life experiences of those persons important to us. Your time frames and focus of experiences may differ from mine. Just be aware of the presence of grace in your life as you review and contemplate your life.

How to Begin
With the Framework or
with the Stories?

*F*or those of you who desire an overview or big picture processing incoming information, I offer a framework with my definitions as they relate to grace and a brief presentation of the facets of grace.

Others of you may initially choose to skip the framework and delve into a fuller explanation of the laws, states, and acts of grace. Next, my life stories illustrating how I came to know and use grace are here to help you create your own big picture from the pieces as the stories unfold. Those pieces may also involve your stories, other theories, supporting data, and your own personal practices. You can return to the framework for clarity and definitions as you contemplate your own grace-filled life.

THE FRAMEWORK
FACETS OF GRACE

*W*ithin this book are specific words that may have meanings attached as the result of cultural and family influences. To help assure that you understand what I mean by creator-of-all, divinity, grace, intention, and signpost in the context of this book, I offer my definitions within this framework for easy reference.

Creator-of-all

Creator-of-all is all the love that can be imagined. All forms and all life dwelling within the world of forms are the creator. And yet the creator is more than that and could be expressed as source choosing to reflect itself as all that love.

The love that exists in our core draws us through an evolutionary process to seek blending and merging with the creator-of-all. This is an evolutionary process that could be called a journey through many forms. This journey takes us back, always expressing more love, to the creator-of-all.

Divinity

Divinity is a force or the power of love, the wellspring of life that gives rise to the world. Divinity is not an exterior force but part of our innate being. Divinity in relationship with the creator-of-all sustains all life.

Grace

Grace, a gift from the creator-of-all, is an organizing force of a higher order available to all life. Grace expresses itself in a set of relationships that work in harmonic resonance for the benefit of all life within and beyond form. Grace manifests its order within each unit of life. Grace results from the relationship of each loving entity to the creator-of-all. Grace emanates from the core of the creator and from the core of each being. Because each being is an extension of life and divinity, each being has access to grace.

Intention

Intention is a purposeful statement generating a spark that ignites an assessable direction for our actions, attitudes, and energy as we move toward a goal or a determined outcome. We state our intention and steadfastly stretch toward manifesting that intention with resolve and determination. We give our intention attention.

Signpost

A signpost serves as an indicator as to the progress we are making in realizing our intention. A signpost is a signal from which to measure the depth of success in stretching toward our goal. A signpost can guide or help direct us and serve as a beacon as we navigate toward living life within the higher order of grace.

Laws of Grace

Interwoven in my story is the framework I have come to know as the laws of grace, the states of grace, and the acts of grace. I identify the laws of grace as three essential principles that define grace as I have come to know it. They represent a way of life within a higher order.

The First Law

Grace expresses divinity and is all-pervasive.

Know it is so.

The Second Law

Grace is interlaced with love, and our role is to surrender.

The Third Law

Grace channels power, and one result of
that power is manifestation.

And so it is.

States of Grace

States of grace are the expressions of those principles within the laws of grace that help us recognize and amplify the presence of grace in our daily lives. The numbers do not imply priority or importance and are simply used as reference to differentiate the states of grace.

First state of grace: it is our **birthright** to call upon grace in relationship with divinity to manifest for the highest good.

Second state of grace: all our intentions are accomplished with **ease** when we align with the divine, the power of love, and surrender.

Third state of grace: **abundance** is experienced when we recognize love is interlaced with grace harmonizing with the creator-of-all and divinity.

Fourth state of grace: we live in **beauty** as love interlaces with all pervasive grace.

Fifth state of grace: **altruism** is the result of claiming our power supported by all-pervasive grace.

Sixth state of grace: to be **receptive**, we surrender to all-pervasive grace.

Seventh state of grace: an **outpouring** is the result of love interlaced with grace and power.

Eighth state of grace: when we surrender to the power of manifesting, we live in **harmony**.

Ninth state of grace: **trust** is possible when divine grace flows with power.

Tenth state of grace: the **golden light** of all-pervasive grace holds and sustains our manifestations for the greater good of all.

Eleventh state of grace: **pure love** is manifested with the interlacing of love and grace.

Twelfth state of grace: surrendering to the power of grace assures **purity** of intent that embraces selfless service for the greater good.

Acts of Grace

The acts of grace are the outstanding outcomes or results of living a graceful life within the laws of grace. Know there is no particular order or priority implied.

First act of grace: manifest the divine.

Second act of grace: clarity

Third act of grace: joy

Fourth act of grace: dimensionality

Fifth act of grace: freedom

Sixth act of grace: synchronicity

Seventh act of grace: radiance

Eighth act of grace: infinity

CHAPTER 1

● ● ● ● ● ● ● ● ● ● ● ● ● ● ● ● ●

Developing a Life Perspective of Unity

I was strapped in my seatbelt as my car was cartwheeling through the air. Through the front windshield, the horizon line kept changing, with the sky on top and then the ground on top. With the third and final cartwheel, my car landed with its wheels on the ground. I had fallen asleep going down the interstate with the cruise control set at seventy-five miles per hour.

A few minutes earlier, I had said to myself, "I am tired." I had good reason to be tired. I was returning from delivering five family members to the airport forty-five miles from the location of our just-completed family reunion. Seventeen of our children and grandchildren had gathered at our South Dakota home for a week in August. I took it upon myself to help provide food, organize gatherings with extended family and friends, help with transportation, and be an energetic, loving mother and grandmother. It was such a joy to be all together, but a great outflow of energy was required on my part.

Just before I was whirling in the air, I heard a voice say loudly, "Loretta, wake up." I was cruising in the median about fifty yards from a drop-off onto the railroad tracks passing under the interstate.

Immediately I turned the wheel in an attempt to return to the blacktop, hit a guard rail, and became airborne.

I said out loud, "Well, here goes!" I surrendered and relaxed my body, observing my arms and hands flailing about. The windows broke out as the front end and then the rear end of my car met the ground with each cartwheel. My seat broke loose on one of these flips, but I stayed belted in the seat within the frame of the car. I remained fully conscious in those moments, not considering living or dying, or any outcome, for that matter. I was truly one with the experience, not focusing on my thoughts and feelings.

The car landed on its wheels three feet from the drop-off to the railroad tracks. I assessed my physical situation. The distortion and rapid bruising of my left forearm led me to think it could be broken. People approached rapidly, and I asked to remain in place until the ambulance arrived. I knew from past experience that I could not evaluate my injuries reliably, as shock often masks symptoms. In my work as a registered nurse in the emergency room, I had helped several patients who had moved out of their vehicles or put off care for several hours following an accident. We often don't feel the extent of our injuries due to the adrenaline rush of stress and perhaps the innate protection of our physical and psychological selves from the full impact of traumatic events.

I tell this story to illustrate the potency of the conscious presence of grace in my life. There was no feeling of fear throughout the ordeal. That fact alone is a confirmation of the presence of grace. The second law of grace is that love is interlaced with grace, and our role is to cooperate and surrender. Fear cannot reside where there is love.

The clarity of my thoughts and actions was a marvel to me. I never questioned my request of the ambulance driver to take me across the bridge over the tracks to the hospital that was a few miles farther than the hospital on the bridge side where my car rested. Only later did I recognize the symbolism of crossing that bridge as well as the command to "wake up" in my spiritual development. I do know everything happens for the highest good within the field of grace. I set the intention that each day I am surrounded by the golden light of grace.

After I was examined in the emergency room, I was declared whole and released to my relieved and loving husband and family. After midnight, a highway patrolman called our house, asked how I was, and said, "She was not alone."

Surprised, Ken said, "What do you mean?"

The patrolman said, "God had to have been with her!"

Another gift was bestowed on me that day with the drama of totaling my car. I went through the entire course of menopause in those few moments. In the following months, I had no irregular menstrual cycles. I experienced no hot flashes, moodiness, or diminishment of sexual desire. There was immediate cessation. I simply moved on to what my Native American friends call the grandmother's lodge. I don't know the meaning behind instantaneous menopause, but at fifty years of age, I appreciated that outcome. I accepted it as part of the whole experience in which I was the recipient of the outpouring of pure love that is grace.

This experience and my reactions within it served to validate my life view that gives meaning and purpose to my daily existence. In general, my life view is one of unity, of oneness, and of connectedness.

At that moment of cartwheeling, I had no consciousness of past or future or thoughts of living or dying. There was only the experience of my car and me hurtling through space. I was one within the order of grace. At that precise time, the divine order called grace held the coherence of love and action most meaningful for my spiritual growth and life path. I was totally present. I was one with the experience, outside thought.

Each of us can move toward a life experience of unity by coming to reside within the higher order or essence of grace. What stands in our way? One obstacle may be our tendency to view and describe our experiences with the attributes of duality. Some examples of duality are judging life experiences as good or evil, helpful or hindering, right or wrong, strong or weak, and encouraging or discouraging. If we continually view life through the lens of duality or, said another way, the extremes of polarity, we will have quite a different life experience than if we imagine specific thoughts and feelings at the center or a neutral point along a continuum. We can examine our perceptions along that continuum extended to the polarities at each end of the continuum. A simple example is white at one polarity and black at the other and all shades of gray in between.

When I want to experience anything more fully, to be more conscious and to evolve spiritually, I engage my divine core by focusing on and breathing into my heart center. I present a question or a concept I am inspired to learn more about. I mentally pull out from the core feelings, words, or images, extending them as a ray of energy. I label the extremes of each end of the ray with words describing those feelings and images. That process allows me to bring forth from the potential of my core—the energy flowing along a continuum that is tangible and available for my knowing and use.

I once counseled with a friend who viewed life from an extreme polarity, giving daily attention to one traumatic aspect of her life. El was distraught over a circumstance she had experienced earlier when her four-month-old son died in his crib. The authorities called it sudden infant death syndrome. Feelings of self-hate seemed to consume her every thought. El was totally identifying with only one aspect of who she was; she saw herself as a negligent mother. As El realized she was narrowing her identity and thinking and acting only from that perspective, she opened her focus to include other roles in which she engaged daily. El identified her roles of wife, mother, attorney, friend, and community member. El then began embracing all the roles with which she identified, and she lightened the impact of her role as a perceived negligent mother or even murderer.

El took another discovery step and extended a continuum as a negligent mother. At one polarity the label "murderer" defined her perception. At the opposite pole, "wise woman" described her action as she chose to move forward with acceptance to preserve life quality for her surviving family.

Much of the confusion and pain we experience comes from becoming stuck or obsessed with only one portion of an extended ray of energy we extract from the whole. My friend El had only identified with the negligent role and the murderer polarity, and thus she felt separated from her center and the vastness of potential that was her.

How can we move between a duality perspective and one of unity in a conscious, meaningful way? To delve even deeper into a life view of unity, we come to realize that even the roles we assume are reflections and aspects of duality emanating from our divine core. Planet earth is our school ground for learning of these potentials and reflections. We are able to draw forth, witness, identify, and co-create with our divine core a life of meaning within the flow of grace. Our core, now in form, is our essential self, containing our purpose and potential, and is also of the unified essence described as the creator-of-all.

The organization or higher order of grace facilitates the realization of our potential and highest life purpose. This higher order of grace is a gift to all life aspects within the world of form. Carolyn Myss, in her CDs *Channeling Grace*, describes grace as "the breath of God." The more we know of grace and live within its order, the more we breathe life in fully with contentment and peace.

The higher order of grace helps make possible the movement from the core of potential into manifesting recognizable events and meaning. The perspective of unity assures us we are all one, only reflecting various qualities extended out from that core of oneness to provide clarity and growth.

Those rays of knowing that reflect duality are greatly affected by our individual and cultural beliefs. Established beliefs and ways of being are defined to serve a specific purpose, but these ways of being are seldom discarded when that purpose is no longer valid.

An example of a norm held within the United States public school systems is currently being challenged. This norm involves attention. How often have we heard, "Pay attention, stay focused, time on task is paramount"? In reality, we are demanding in our classrooms the development of one extreme of the energy ray of attention. Attention can slide along the continuum from a pinpoint of focused attention to an all-inclusive sense of connectedness with no particular object of focus.

Years ago I learned the technique of "Open Focus," which allows me to slide along the continuum of attention, stopping where it best suits the immediate situation and what is best for me. Simply knowing of this attention continuum or any other continuum gives us freedom and permission to acknowledge the extremes of polarity and all the choices in between those extremes. Schools that promote rest or daydream time, play, yoga, and meditation are now extending that narrow focus of attention toward a more open focus.

As we return to our core and the perspective of unity, we invoke and accept the freedom offered by the gift of grace. Each application or invocation of grace aids in the resolution of karmic consequences. A simple explanation of karma as it is used in this context implies an individual has acted outside the higher order of grace where the pure love of the creator-of-all is reflected. Karma draws out the extremes, helping to identify the cause and effect resulting from choices of actions taken. I am proposing that grace offers us an opportunity to expand our belief beyond the "cause and effect" belief associated with karma to include a belief of unity with a lively connection to our divine core and an insight into how all is interconnected.

Experiencing Grace involves the expansion of consciousness of self to all of one's surroundings as an unbroken whole, a consciousness of awe from which negative mind states are absent, from which healing and groundedness result. For these reasons Grace has long been deemed "amazing."

—Charlene Spretnak

CHAPTER 2

Defining the Laws of Grace

The three laws of grace are at once both simple and profound. As we acknowledge and live by these laws, our life is blessed. We experience a life vision of unity.

- First law—grace expresses divinity and is all pervasive.

- Second law—grace interlaces with love, and our role is to surrender.

- Third law—grace channels power, and one result of that power is manifestation.

The order of grace makes tangible our knowing the ultimate love that is the creator-of-all. Through the yearning to know the pure love and unity that is the creator-of-all, we bring forth or "will" the presence of grace. Grace is the organizing force within and beyond form we call forth from source, the creator-of-all.

As human forms, we touch, see, hear, smell, taste, and intuit the dynamic qualities of other humans, nature, and ourselves. Within the order of grace, we recognize that we are connected. We are divine expressing the power of love. We are powerful in recognizing or manifesting what is needed for the highest good. One way to recognize the order of grace is to reflect upon and hold in consciousness the laws of grace.

Grace is a powerful tool for knowing oneself, for recognizing our connection to the universe and beyond, and for personal growth and transformation. The presence of grace is tangible or intangible and within or outside our level of awareness. It is our choice to bring this omnipresent divine order into awareness, making it tangible and of greater use. Bringing this natural organization of life into awareness is a necessary first step to recognize and activate grace in our daily lives.

The First Law

Grace expresses divinity and is all-pervasive. Know it is so.

Recognizing Grace often begins with faith; accepting and believing certain precepts. As youngsters, we live within family and culture. We are asked to consider and maybe even adopt a spiritual path and cultural norms that direct our thoughts and actions. We are asked to absorb and trust these teaching as truth. As a young person, my parents took me to the Roman Catholic Church. The Ten Commandments directed my behavior. The idea of sin and its consequences set the boundaries of what I chose to do. Also, respecting my parents and their rules figured into my decision making.

Around the age of ten, I stole a pack of Kool cigarettes from my parents' store and proceeded to smoke in the outhouse behind the store. Later my father used the outhouse and sought me out, asking if I had smoked in there. I quickly said no. He accepted that answer. I felt guilty and ashamed of myself. (I definitely realized not to count on my actions ever being a secret!) Further, I learned it felt lousy to steal and then to lie, dishonoring my father. I credit living within the order of grace for giving me the ability to discern those qualities of truth and respect that felt right and made me feel good as a ten-year-old.

Not only did these Christian beliefs help connect me with the organization of grace within my young life, but the Native American path of my friends augmented that sense of order and harmony I know as grace. The Native spirituality instilled in me the connectedness of all of life.

In the fall following the first freeze, I would walk the creek beds with friends searching for wild turnips, *timsula* in Lakota, to add to stew made with beef or buffalo. We would shake the bushes to release the buffalo berries we used to cook buffalo berry syrup and jelly. The act of using the nourishing gifts of the prairies was considered ceremony within the Lakota community and was approached with reverence and gratitude. During each ceremony we continually uttered "*Mitakuye oyasin,*" translated as, "All my relations."

I also came to know, in the Lakota tradition, that the needs and accomplishments of an individual should never take precedence over the collective group or tribal needs and recognition. This fact of not standing out as an individual came to the forefront during one Christmas when we were living and working at Takini School on the Cheyenne River Sioux Indian Reservation in the center of South Dakota. An eight-year-old student, Wanbli, was the topic of a book titled *A Boy Becomes a Man at Wounded Knee,* by Ted Wood with Wanbli Numpa Afraid of Hawk. This book chronicled the grueling 150-mile horseback ride retracing the trail taken by the Lakota people in 1890 that ended in their massacre at Wounded Knee, South Dakota. The narration and photos of the journey were poignant. They told of the mending of the sacred hoop and the healing of the spirit of the people. The direct descendants of the Lakota people who were massacred were students, parents, and staff present at the school. A hardback copy of this book was given as a gift to all three hundred-plus students, but only with the permission of the elders after they deemed it was more about the tribe than the one boy.

These two spiritual traditions, Christian beliefs and Native American spirituality, were not at odds within my early development. In fact, I know from hearing early childhood stories from many friends that I had a broader and less literal interpretation of rules and expectations. Even as a preteenager, I questioned authoritative proclamations of what was right or wrong. Living connected with nature, I recognized the goodness and the interplay that supported my young life. I intuitively recognized what was of value to me. I was not outwardly rebellious but simply discounted quietly what didn't fit my knowing.

Our spiritual paths, along with family and cultural structures, offer us our earliest knowledge of the order of grace that is always present within and beyond form. Then, as we mature, we come to know our personal truths through our life studies and experiences. Accepting the order of grace, we recognize relationships or patterns that work in harmony for the benefit of all life.

The Second Law

Grace interlaces with love, and our role is to surrender.

Grace is the result of the harmonic relationship between all loving essences and the creator-of-all. Grace is a carrier of love. Love focuses grace. Grace amplifies love. To know grace is to know love. When we experience love, we experience grace. Grace is eternally present waiting to be channeled into our awareness.

If the second law of grace says our role is to surrender, just what does it mean to "surrender?" Surrender implies a willingness to give up isolation and accept partnership with the divine. So often in my life I have thought, "I have to do it and not count on anyone else." This was especially true regarding my experience with our five children, born within a seven-year time span. I often fell into bed at night feeling exhausted and sometimes unappreciated. Even though my husband was willing to pitch in and follow my directions, it wasn't enough. I expected Ken to read my mind and anticipate my need for more help. I remember thinking, "If he can't see that I need help, then I'll do it myself." I seldom asked for support and often ended up feeling alone or isolated.

As our children grew and I matured, I realized I couldn't control all our lives. I surrendered to the fact that daily routine and even important decisions needed to be shared by those involved. However, it felt like I was shirking my responsibility as a wife and mother. In reflection, I know I confused my knowingness of responsibility and of control. At times I thought I was being responsible, and I was really controlling. Now I know that I did not fully accept my own divinity, meaning I didn't trust that power of love within myself and my husband and children. By the time our five children were teenagers, I surrendered control. I truly accepted the fact that each of us was a divine being and capable of making responsible, loving choices.

I had to realize that surrender, either through necessity or wisdom or both, is to give up exclusive control and accept shared control. I partnered with the divine, the power of love, in the intimate process of control. In partnering with the divine, I honor my own needs and recognize that the needs of all are considered worthy of my love and action.

In psychological terms, I recognize and even befriend my shadow side that is energized by the feelings of fear and isolation. In surrendering, I allow the shadow to transform or come into the light by modeling love for it and introducing it to the light. The shadow is that part of myself I struggle to acknowledge. My shadow could be laziness, cowardice, pride, selfishness, or even security. My own shadow has involved sadness, almost to the point of despair. Twice it has come forth from deep within me with sobbing that lasted for nearly an hour each time. Each of the triggers rationally seemed unrelated to the depth of despair I experienced.

I was in my forties when this shadow first appeared. The trigger was being stranded at the local library after 11:00 p.m. We lived ten miles from town. I had been dropped off for an evening meeting. I waited to be picked up after the meeting and called home twice before 11:00 p.m. We were on an eight-party telephone line, and others would pick up. I decided to be a victim and not ask these neighbors for help. After all, Ken should figure out I needed a ride. Finally at 2:00 a.m., I called a friend in town to come and get me and take me home. I was angry at being abandoned. Ken was sleeping in our bed. He was surprised at my anger, since he thought I was out with friends and would get a ride home. Ken held me for the hour as I sobbed from the depth of my being, allowing all feeling to dissolve and to finally come to peaceful quietness.

The second trigger still seems unrelated to the depth of despair it conjures up within me. The trigger is the movie *Dances with Wolves*. Yes, I grew up on the Cheyenne River Sioux Indian Reservation where the movie was filmed. But rationally that fact alone cannot account for the deep pain and sadness I experience with the mere thought of that movie to this day. I hold myself and my connections with the Lakota people in the golden light of grace. I ask to surrender this shadow experience into the loving presence of grace.

The phrase "Ask and it shall be given unto you" comes brightly to the forefront in this law. When surrendering our sense of isolation and asking to experience the connection with the divine, we invite grace. With that grace comes love, the experience of unity and the wisdom to serve where needed. May we hold the intention to invoke grace and surrender to the loving potential of the creator-of-all.

The Third Law

Grace channels power and one result of
that power is manifestation.

And so it is.

Grace brings its order in relationship with the creator-of-all and the force of love into each life and unit of consciousness. As we immerse ourselves in the golden light of grace, we channel the power that is our birthright. Imagine intention as a divine spark that generates form. If we are aligned with our life purpose, our intentions are manifested, or recognized effortlessly. The initiator of the thought or intention reaps the consequences of those intentions.

To grasp the reality of manifesting our intentions, it may be helpful to imagine all life forms as expressions of thoughts and desires precipitated from an infinite pool of possibilities. We have only to use the power spoken of in this third law of grace, to ask from that part of ourselves that is aligned with our soul's purpose and to trust our worthiness to recognize and receive what we desire.

Manifesting, or becoming aware of the presence of what we desire, is simple when we are invoking the organizing force of grace. Yet our human experience can establish boundaries of what is possible. These boundaries can be promoted by families, friends, and cultures. We can adhere to a dualistic view or a belief that we are separate from our environment and from our source. Often we must relearn that we are divine; we are one with all, and all is available.

I notice within my own life that I am sometimes careful, even timid, regarding what I ask to be manifested. I question, "Is this because I think of scarcity? Do I believe there is a scarcity or limit as to what I am worthy of receiving? Do I believe in a self-fulfilling prophecy of limited resources? Or do I choose my petitions carefully, asking this question: what will promote my life purpose and everyday experience of joy and love?" Each of us must determine whether we are careful out of scarcity thinking or out of discernment.

I do admit that I turn thoughts or proclamations into manifestation from semiconscious, even playful, awareness. On several occasions I have made a statement of what I wanted, and it comes about without further thought. In retrospect, I usually view the event of manifestation with astonishment and smiles from the inside out.

You will read of several of these manifestations in the stories that follow. One manifestation I include here as an example. Fourteen years ago during a winter visit to Arizona, I proclaimed to my husband, Ken, that I wanted to live in Sedona, and, furthermore, I wanted to live in a home built by my favorite creative builder Monty Wilson. Ken just looked at me with no comment. We were in love with living in the Black Hills of South Dakota for over twenty years. Besides that, we did not have the financial means to purchase a Monty home. I had declared the desire or intention, put the how-tos in the background and went about daily living with very little thought of the desire.

The amazing fact is that now, fourteen years later, we live in Sedona and in a Monty home. I really had surrendered the specifics of how and when this would be manifested. Although I was surprised, there was a part of me that never doubted it would happen.

I give thanks every day that I live within the force of grace and am humbled when acknowledging the power I share as a divine being in this benevolent universe. Each of us has this power.

"We have all been told that grace is to be found in the universe. But in our human foolishness and short-sightedness we imagine divine grace to be finite. For this reason we tremble ... But the moment comes when our eyes are opened and we see and realize that grace is infinite. Grace, my friends, demands nothing from us but that we shall await it with confidence and acknowledge it in gratitude. Grace, my friends, makes no conditions and singles out none of us in particular; grace takes us all to its bosom and proclaims general amnesty."

—Osak Denisen

· · · · · · · · · · · · · · · · ·

CHAPTER 3

Coming to Know the States of Grace

The Expressions of Grace in Our Lives

I *am coming to know twelve* states of grace as I consciously apply the laws of grace in my life. Each state or expression of grace is represented as a single word highlighted within the intention. I offer the following states of grace as intentions to enhance the expression of grace in your daily life and include summarizing signposts to help you recognize that you are living a grace-filled life.

Our **birthright** is to call upon grace in relationship with divinity to manifest for the highest good.

As conscious life forms, we have the right to call upon the natural organization of life in harmony with the power of love to manifest what we desire and need. First we realize we do not have to earn or merit the presence of grace in our lives. Grace just is. Second, grace's order becomes more apparent and powerful as we intentionally ask to be more conscious of grace, moment to moment. Some ways we do this are to pray, to meditate, to invoke, and to develop rituals.

Some detriments to experiencing the full expression of grace that I have encountered are the illusion that I am "not worthy," as well as a duality life view, that is, my interpretation of actions from a cause-and-effect model. Examples include: if I choose not to volunteer, I will be thought selfish; or I need to accept every offer of friendship so I won't find myself alone and unloved.

Other semiconscious habits such as judging, defensive rationalizations, and protective postures have developed in me as the result of family, community, and cultural input. Perhaps the consideration of "shoulds," "appropriateness" and the thought, "if I don't watch out for myself, who will?" hold back my full participation in grace. I feel vulnerable or even wounded, pulling back in fear and doubt instead of expanding into the love of grace. These habits have clouded my immersion within the natural order of a grace-filled daily existence. I can't help but smile when I recognize the misplaced effort I can expend when I ignore or forget the availability of grace that is my birthright.

Intention: As my birthright, I call upon grace to manifest my intention for the highest good.

Signpost: Without the perception that we earned the presence of grace, we fully recognize that we are supported with the love and guidance we know as grace.

When we align with the divine, the power of love, and surrender, all our intentions are accomplished with **ease**.

Our intentions are manifested effortlessly as we surrender and accept full partnership with the divine, the power of love. For me, partnering or sharing control with divinity involves gratitude and humility. My intentions, manifesting easily, engender such magnanimous feelings and a sense of awe. The action of setting the intention and releasing, or "Let go, let God," feels like a giant spiraling whirlpool feeding itself and growing more powerful as it spins.

I offer our knowing of gratitude and humility as an example of a strong sense or feeling upon which we can enlarge to accomplish manifesting our intentions with ease. When I experience gratitude, my heart is open, and I move within a field of love, fully validated and supported. I know a heartfelt "thank you" is sufficient. With humility, I recognize that I am part of a greater whole, a perfect love that requires that I leave fears behind and live from a good and gracious place with patience and acceptance.

Intention: All my intentions are accomplished with ease as I align with divinity and surrender.

Signpost: Life flows without strife, and we say, "That was easy."

Abundance is experienced when we recognize that love is interlaced with grace harmonizing with divinity.

The natural organization of life interwoven with love and infused with the force of that love creates abundance and beauty. Abundance is a state of mind where we know we will have what we need when we need it. We have a choice to believe in a model of scarcity or a model of abundance. That belief is generally formed by how readily our basic needs have been met, or, more accurately, how we have perceived that our needs have been met in the past or are being met now. Anguish is the result of thinking there is only so much of anything, and we must get our share. Hoarding, competition, fear, and even violence may result from adopting the scarcity model.

When we live within the laws of grace, we experience love, and we know we are provided for. Our needs are met. If the idea of abundance does not seem a reality in our daily lives, let us pay attention to our thoughts and words. Most likely we have adopted certain limitations of which we are not even conscious. Habits, prejudices, personality traits, and family patterns all promote ways of unconsciously interpreting what we are continually experiencing. These limitations or expectations may well be keeping our intentions of abundance from manifesting.

Intention: I experience abundance as I recognize love is interlaced with grace harmonizing with divinity.

Signpost: We feel we live in a benevolent world, and worry about the future is minimized or absent.

We live in **beauty** as love interlaces with all pervasive grace.

With focus on the present, the gifts offered by nature and by much that comprises our encounters, we cannot help but experience beauty. If the saying "Beauty lies in the eyes of the beholder," is correct, our sense of beauty is cultivated from within. We come to perceive the beauty within ourselves and then experience that beauty reflected in the world about us. For me, beauty includes the qualities of peace, balance, and appreciation.

When I observe a baby sleeping on its back with its abdomen rising and falling with each easy breath and the tiny mouth muscles twitching in a sucking motion, I know I am observing the beauty of developing life. I invite that ease and peace to wash over me as I match those abdominal breaths. I truly unite with that beauty and experience the outpouring of grace and love present. The hassle and consternation of daily life swirling around me evaporate in the act of appreciating and uniting with that sleeping baby who is gracing my presence. We must seek and recognize beauty amid the chaos within the exterior and interior worlds in which we reside. We do have control of our perspective and interpretation because we are conscious beings.

Intention: I live in beauty as love is interlaced with all-pervasive grace.

Signpost: We appreciate the minute and the magnificent qualities of the encounters in our daily lives.

> "I look forward to an America which will
> not be afraid of Grace and beauty."
>
> —John F. Kennedy

Altruism is the result of claiming our power supported by all-pervasive Grace.

We are altruistic as we engage the set of relationships called grace, combined with the power of love that works in harmonic resonance for the benefit of all. Altruism recognizes all are equal. In other words, no one is worth more than anyone else. We engage altruism by adopting a selfless concern for the welfare of others, when we seek common good over private good, and when we do good without the expectation of reward or recognition. The power of grace assures us we come from a selfless, altruistic base in our thoughts and actions.

Intention: I claim my power supported by all-pervasive grace, and I am altruistic.

Signpost: We give and receive without expectation and recognition.

To be **receptive**, we surrender to all-pervasive grace.

Sharing control with the force of love within the natural organization of a Grace-filled life promotes receptivity to greater pure love, beauty, and abundance. Receptivity is the capacity to open to, to absorb, and to hold the qualities of omnipresent grace.

Intention: I surrender to all-pervasive grace, and I am receptive.

Signpost: We are open, without fear, to explore and adopt new patterns of behavior and thought if deemed beneficial.

An **outpouring** or giving force is the result of love interlaced with grace and power.

As love is interlaced with the natural organization of life known as grace and powered with the force of love, we experience an outpouring of all the expressions of grace upon ourselves and all requests (who or whatever else is) included in our invocations.

Intention: I experience an outpouring or giving force as the result of love interlaced with grace and power.

Signpost: We experience feeling fully supported and a flooding sense of well-being as we move through our daily lives.

When we surrender to the power of manifesting, we live in **harmony**.

Harmony is that fine line of balance we create continually by combining our intentions to manifest with the power of love. We know harmony when we experience the balance and coherence of thought and action. We are happy, energetic, and poised as we release our intentions to become manifested. With harmony, we live naturally and unselfishly in our complex world.

Intention: I live in harmony as I surrender to the power of creating.

Signpost: We feel confident in our decisions and maintain a balance between doing and letting or, said another way, rowing and flowing.

Grace has been defined as the outward expression
of the inward harmony of the Soul.

—William Hazlitt

Trust is possible when divine grace flows with power.

Trust is a way of living knowing fully the power imparted by the force of love within the higher order of life that is our birthright. We know we are loved and valued and have faith all is in order.

Intention: Trust is possible when grace flows within the power of love.

Signpost: We fearlessly pursue our dreams knowing we are protected and guided.

The **golden light** of all-pervasive grace holds and sustains our manifestation for the greater good of all.

A surefire way to illumine the natural organization of life and to manifest altruistic expressions is to invoke the golden light of grace. Simply ask that the golden light be showered upon self, others, and our planetary being. Grace illuminates, lifts, and supports.

Intention: The golden light of all-pervasive grace sustains my manifestations for the greater good of all.

Signpost: We feel surrounded with love and possibilities and the support is tangible.

Pure love is manifested with the interlacing of love and grace.

An example of pure love is benevolent empathy with other essences. We can intuit what another is experiencing both by understanding on a cognitive level and by feeling the experience as compassion. That compassion inspires altruism for the benefit of a shared global community organized by divine grace.

Intention: Pure love is manifesting with the interlacing of love and grace.

Signpost: We are not separated and alone. We feel connected and uplifted.

Surrendering to the power of grace assures **purity** of intent that embraces selfless service.

Grace clarifies and makes pure. Purity is openness without pretense or protective behaviors. Purity is the state of trusting, knowing, and acting with conviction that all is in right order. Purity is radiant with pure love—a radiance that glows and engulfs life in an inspirational flow of love and light. We can live our daily lives carried along in the glowing flow of purity.

I recognize that I am experiencing the state of grace I call purity when my intentions manifest with ease. I have surrendered and feel supported as I accept this pure, unconditional love that is my birthright.

Intention: I surrender to the power of grace that assures purity of intent that embraces selfless service.

Signpost: Motivation and action are above questioning and reproach.

I invite you to identify specific states or expressions of grace in your daily life and consider which laws of grace you are presently embracing. With that awareness, you can consciously expand the expressions of grace and live more fully within the flow of grace.

The state of grace is a condition in which all growth is effortless, a transparent, joyful acquiescence that is the general requirement of all existence ... You are born in the state of grace; it is impossible for you to leave it. You will die in a state of grace ... you cannot "fall out of grace," nor can it be taken from you.

—Jane Robert

CHAPTER 4

• • • • • • • • • • • • • • • •

Presenting the Acts of Grace

The Results of Grace in Our Lives

The eight acts of grace are the result of applying the laws of grace. These acts of grace are the concrete outcomes or consequences of living a conscious or even unconscious existence within the laws of grace. Before I personally identified or came to know the laws of grace, I was cognizant of the thoughts and behaviors that I now identify as acts of grace. As you read vignettes from my life story in the next chapters, you will see and feel how the empowering acts of grace led me to know and define the laws and states of grace. I invite you to identify specific outcomes or results of grace you've observed within your own experiences and follow them back to pinpoint the states and laws of grace that were present. This action will boost your ongoing active participation with grace in all aspects of your life.

First Act of Grace: Manifestation

Manifestation is the result of living our lives within the organization of grace. Perhaps a more accurate word to describe manifestation is recognition. We manifest or recognize our intentions as the result of invoking grace interlaced with love and by claiming the power of grace to manifest. May it be our intention to align ourselves with our soul's purpose. May we recognize that we are expressing our divinity when we have no fear, only joy, as we recognize the power of love in acceptance. We have limitless abundance in our lives when invoking grace for the highest good for self and others.

I do not plan the specifics of how my life is to unfold. Thankfully I recognized my husband of fifty-plus years as the love of my life when he first appeared. Together we have supported each other as we let life happen. Joy and love multiplied as each of our five children joined our family. We were at times in awe of how money, job opportunities, food, friends, and answers manifested when and where most needed. We trust in the benevolence present in our world and continue to be humbled and grateful to live within the order of grace.

This manifestation of our intentions can occur outside our expectation of time lines or circumstances. Our recognition of the fulfillment of our desires may be obscured by our expectations of how and when. To fully experience the manifestations of the intentional spark we ignite in the pool of infinite potential, we focus, surrender, and receive or recognize what we have consciously or unconsciously called forth. For most people, manifesting, or recognizing the divine, is foremost in soul's purpose. We are capable of creating heaven on earth. One way of describing heaven is the ability to live in a caring, supportive environment where we are valued and loved for that divine self we are.

In manifesting the divine, we continually carry the intention that all our thoughts and actions are for the highest good of all as we focus on the value and potential in all life. This benevolent attitude results in altruistic actions. Acts of altruism are the result of our devotion to the welfare of others where we truly feel an unselfish concern for others.

The presence of grace in our lives can be recognized and defined. When we observe our actions and listen to the response of others to these actions, we may hear phrases such as, "You're an angel," "You seem to glow," "You are divine," and "You light up the room."

We manifest the divine as love permeates all we think and do, every thought and every action. We affirm love of self and, most assuredly, love of all creation.

Second Act of Grace: Clarity

Clarity is an act or outcome of grace present in our lives. When applying the laws of grace, clarity of thought and action results when we accept and surrender to the powerful presence of grace. We surrender our fears and uncertainties. We are confident about our decisions. We act with purpose and discernment. There is no second-guessing. Even now as I describe the outcomes of grace, I am receptive, and I invoke the golden light of grace. When I write with confidence and with clarity, that clarity then leads to ease of understanding. May the concept and value of grace be illuminated and be made clear as you accept a grace-filled life.

An example of clarity in my life still defies explanation except that I was open to the next adventure. At thirty-nine years of age I was ready for a new challenge. Our five children were all teenagers and well on their way to being conscious, healthy adults. Now it was my turn to step up, contribute to the larger society, and turn my attention to my own spiritual evolvement in a clear, concise way.

During our first twenty years of marriage, as we raised our five children, I also obtained bachelor of science degrees in biology and education. Attending school at the same time as raising a family was possible because I was in charge of my schedule. That experience and education led to developing innovative education programs, which provided me a platform as a consultant and as a keynote and workshop speaker. I presented research and built a reputation as a leader in the study of biofeedback and wellness when these concepts first were recognized as tools within the public school.

A friend encouraged me to obtain a graduate degree, and one summer morning he proceeded to open a door for me so this could happen. I clearly knew the field of study would be psychophysiology with an emphasis on the transpersonal aspect of psychology.

Within two months, my graduate committee was in place, and an outline of program courses with adjunct professors was accepted. I packed my car, left home and family, and immersed myself in this growth opportunity for the next two years. I clearly acted on my calling, and with clarity, ease, and support from my family, I stepped into this grand adventure within the order of grace.

Third Act of Grace: Joy

When we experience joy, we are experiencing an act of grace. Joy wells up within us, and our eyes tear up when we are immersed in the manifestations of love interlaced with all-pervasive grace. That sense of support and love gives us the ability to care for the welfare of others with abandon. We feel rewarded and powerful.

We may at times describe the experience of joy as blissful. We experience bliss when our hearts are open to the love present because we know we are connected to and supported by the totality of creation.

Even today I vividly recall strolling on the boardwalk along the beach during a visit to Southern California. I was with my two favorite men, my husband, Ken, and my friend Leo. The sunset was shades of orange and red. A sailboat moved across the horizon. We were silent and transfixed, experiencing the joy, the elation and the wonder of such beauty and love. That moment was a gift beyond expression, and our tears flowed freely in wonderment and gratitude.

When we live in grace, we live in joy. When that sense of joy retreats to the background, and fear and suffering come to the forefront, we can invoke grace. We can call upon the golden light of grace to sustain the positive intentions we put forth for ourselves, for others, and for situations.

One late fall evening, Ken and I snuggled up with joy and contentment alone in the home we shared with our son David and daughter-in-law Cori. David had gone to the Big Horn Mountains of Wyoming and set up camp for the weekend. Cori was driving by herself to join him. About 10:00 p.m., David called to ask what time Cori had left. A blizzard with zero visibility had hit the Big Horns, and she should have arrived by the time he called. He tried to drive the steep mountain trails to locate her pickup, but he was unsuccessful. He called us back again to see if she had called us. We realized then that there was limited cell reception in the mountains. David's panic was escalating, and in his increasing concern he was endangering his own life attempting to drive the steep passes. Sitting at home, we felt fear and a sense of helplessness. David called one last time near midnight, saying he was staying at camp until the light of day. Ken and I realized the situation was out of our control, and together we prayed for protection and for the golden light of grace to surround our family. Knowing of the presence of grace and the power of calling it forth eased our fear, and we finally slept. At 6:00 a.m., we were awakened by the telephone. It was Cori. She had gotten stuck in a snowdrift and stayed with the pickup for the night. When daybreak came, she had hiked up a narrow road until her cell phone worked. She then called us immediately. Cori gave us landmarks to guide David to her. Within minutes, David called, and we relayed the information. We were all crying with joy and relief. Knowing of the presence of grace and the power of calling it forth had eased our fear. It was a dramatic lesson in surrendering and trusting in love and grace.

Fourth Act of Grace: Dimensionality

As we surrender our need to control and as we partner with the divine, we possess the power to experience the interconnection of all life, both within and beyond form. We identify with our own personal makeup—our physical, mental, emotional, and spiritual dimensions. Expanding beyond self, an outcome of grace for the individual and for the collective culture is to know and experience grace across dimensions.

Perhaps it is not necessary to be aware of the dimensional aspects of grace to reap its benefits. Yet, an outcome or act of grace is the awareness of that interconnection and the dimensionality aspect of our reality. Knowledge provides power. Experience provides wisdom and illumination.

Many models of dimensionality exist. One model is offered here to illustrate the profound workings of grace. We human beings express far more than human consciousness. This model identifies the other levels of expression as well—elemental, devic, mental, and causal consciousness.

Grace at the elemental level supports intention emerging into form, followed by joy in being. At the elemental level, we rejoice in the ability to reproduce and transform. We tap into the very essence of nature. Most Native Americans live as tribes using this essence of nature for insight and survival.

Ceremonial trances open us to other dimensions. At Pine Ridge,

South Dakota, I had the privilege to meet Frank Fools Crow, a Teton ceremonial chief. In my understanding, Fools Crow would heal by calling upon the elementals and the power of *Wakan Tanka*, the Great Spirit. Fools Crow followed the simple ritual of purification and being a hollow bone, connecting with the power and allowing that power to flow through him to answer the prayers or intentions of those seeking his intercession. Fools Crow said we all have natural power, and, with spiritual knowledge, we can connect with greater power and set it into motion. He said we must trust and call in the power. Within the context of this book and the organization we call grace, we say we invoke, surrender, and cooperate with the power of love called divinity, setting that power in motion to fulfill our intentions.

Our family was invited to attend an *inipi*, or sweat lodge ceremony, followed by a *yuwipi* for healing and protection performed by a protégé of Fools Crow. During both ceremonies, the elementals supported our intentions coming into form as sparks that danced throughout the space. In that long night on a mesa outside of Pine Ridge, we felt we were experiencing a primal force, birthing powerful intentions coming into form.

Grace at the devic level assists us in recognizing responsibility and cooperation. Grace promotes leadership and action where a need is perceived. Two dramatic examples of establishing partnerships with the devic beings of substance come to mind. The Native American Holy Man who assumes responsibility for the people of his community intercedes with the devic forces in a particular area and calls in rain to nourish the land. He establishes a partnership with the devic beings of substance, and we say a "rain dance" is performed.

I had a personal encounter with the devic forces. One spring day in the Black Hills of South Dakota, I decided to record the soothing sounds of a creek running by our home. As I taped the sounds for at least twenty minutes, I sat blissfully noticing the smells, sounds, shadows, and the brook trout lazing in the sun's rays just under the surface of the water. When I listened to the recording I couldn't believe my ears. I clearly heard the words, "Now is the time ..." The continuing message seemed speeded up and unintelligible. I played it for two other people, and all agreed we needed to slow the recording to ascertain the full message. Before we did that, the message faded over the next two weeks, and all that remained was the sound of water washing over rocks as it flowed along. Throughout the years, I have recognized the call to action, "Now is the time," and especially now as I write my knowing of grace.

We can intercede with the devic kingdom to seek advice and work cooperatively with our environment. We ask that grace open that dimensionality and interconnectedness that is available to awaken the fullness of life.

Grace can be invoked as well at the human level. Grace helps consciousness to evolve and gives us the opportunity to acknowledge our divinity. We then experience love and can choose to share our divinity and love.

St Francis of Assisi continues to be a timeless inspiration of a being on the human level choosing to share love. St. Francis denounced a life of riches to imitate the life of Christ. He founded and sought recruits to the Franciscan Order, dedicated to the needs of people, animals, and nature. St. Francis himself experienced the results of dimensionality. Perhaps the best example is when he received the stigmata, during a vision of a six-winged angel. The stigmata, or marks resembling the five wounds of Christ, were visible the rest of his earthly life.

To this day, statues of St. Francis of Assisi with birds, and sometimes animals at his feet, adorn our gardens and courtyards. In 1950, the movie *The Flowers of St. Francis*, directed by Rossellini and cowritten with Fellini, depicts many of the stories of love and service attributed to St. Francis.

At the mental level, grace facilitates our creative abilities in relationship with the devic kingdom. Grace aids us in recognizing our realities and clarifying our purpose.

Although I was not aware of just why I was doing it at the time, I committed several years and many resources to fully learn and then teach the three dimensional organizing tool known as Genesa. The concept of Genesa was brought forth by Dr. Derald Langham. This dynamic matrix, a powerful creative tool for me at the mental level, became my preferred method of tapping into master thought forms and for coming to know my truth. The laws, states, and acts of grace are presented within the Genesa matrix to help bring grace to the forefront as a tool for all of us.

Grace at the causal level can be experienced as an infusion to protect and inspire us. We come to know the most efficient and direct expression of the grace we invoke.

Mohandas (Mahatma) Gandhi serves as a present-day example of an inspired life dedicated to service with the compassion of Gautama Buddha and the passion of Christ. Gandhi's life purpose, or, it could be said, soul's purpose, was directly expressed as his actions were guided by his principles of truth and nonviolence.

This model of dimensionality may well be a major avenue of transformation. Using this model, we draw upon the higher or formless levels of being, including mental and causal levels, and involve those levels of being in the lower expression or formed levels of life essence, the human, devic, and elemental levels. Thus we literally link spirit and form and recognize the interconnectedness or unity.

As we live in grace, we experience an existence larger than the reality supported by our physical senses. In fact, our senses serve as a filter allowing only a certain experience of reality. For example, the ability to see or perceive within certain wave lengths of the light spectrum or hear only those vibrations of a narrow bandwidth, limits sensory input and can define a specific reality.

Knowledge and experiences of dimensionality include dreams, near death experiences, observing auras or energy halos surrounding forms, and intuiting a message or happening far away or in the future.

Other possible models to describe dimensionality include multiverse theories such as parallel universes and dimensions where time or space is not a given. To further explore the outcome of dimensionality, quantum physics is a present-day study attempting to explain relationships between matter and energy, or the wave-particle duality. Claude Swanson's *The Synchronized Universe: New Science of the Paranormal* offers a clear accounting of breakthrough physics of energy medicine, healing, and quantum consciousness.

Fifth Act of Grace: Freedom

Freedom is an act of grace. We accept the freedom to analyze and act on our own promptings and urgings. Freedom allows us to step out and step back without the criticism that diminishes our exploratory nature. Freedom involves our ability to describe our experience without being affected by the possibility of our own personal criticism or criticism from others that could negate the value of that experience. Freedom encourages us to acknowledge our actions for what they are and not deny or label those actions for what they should or could be. When we experience what we manifest by surrendering or accepting a partnership with the divine, we know that we make decisions that are most beneficial in the big picture. We are free from doubt. Our insecurities and fears drop away as we realize we are not isolated. We are interconnected and supported by all of creation.

When I left home at thirty-eight years of age, and with five teenagers still at home, I was free—free of the responsibility of daily living with a large family, free to pursue the education and experiences I wanted as an individual, and free of guilt and of what might happen with family relationships. With the full support from my husband and our young adults and with confidence and within the order of grace, I knew this decision was best for all involved. We all recognized now is the time. I felt strongly that I was modeling the freedom available for our teenage children as they chose to live a grace-filled life.

Grace assists us in transcending indoctrination that limits us and induces our fear as a type of guidance or control. These limitations may serve a purpose to protect and challenge us at various points in our lives. But we must think and act beyond those structures. By fully claiming our potential and purpose, we truly brighten and strengthen our individual threads woven into the tapestry of life.

Sixth Act of Grace: Synchronicity

As an outcome of power and love interlaced with all pervasive grace, synchronicity is the act of seemingly unrelated concepts or events coming together in a meaningful manner. We cannot explain this by simple cause and effect.

Synchronistic occurrences enrich our lives and whatever touches our lives. These happenings result in excitement and provide inspiration to explore further and question the status quo. When it is recognized, synchronicity provides an avenue of awareness. It leads to a breakthrough of old, established boundaries that limit new possibilities. When love interlaces with the power of grace, we can manifest the previously unknown through synchronistic events.

Two of my dear friends told me of a synchronistic event they experienced. One morning Jackie shared with Kathy that she was ready for a teacher to guide her development in the area of photography. She mentioned the name of a renowned photographer as a possible teacher for her. That same day, they traveled twenty miles to a deep well in the canyon to collect pure drinking water. At the well, filling his water jugs at that very time was the very same photographer whom Jackie had identified earlier.

Peruse your own memory for times when two or more seemingly unrelated thoughts or events clicked. Together they offered a whole new awareness or possibility. Is your life different now in some way because of these events or concepts coming together? This is outside of the cause-and-effect realm. This is the sixth act of grace—synchronicity.

Seventh Act of Grace: Radiance

Living in radiance and being a radiant presence to others is an outcome of grace. As divinity is imbued in form, the power of love radiates from the form. When divinity, grace, and power come forth, an outpouring of creativity, the light of soul and a force for good is experienced as radiance by all life essences.

Such radiance lights our way and lifts our spirits. We experience radiance in others especially as a flow of light from their eyes that touches our heart. We experience radiance as sparkles or a glow around another or a sky of shimmering color. I have stood in a field of wild flowers and breathed in the radiance. Sometimes when I've approached a child, I've seen and felt the presence of radiant light. A wave of radiance can sweep us up, and we know the divine light being that we are.

"Radiance is an expression of the mysterious way in which
the universe cannot contain the magnificence it houses."

—Brian Swimmer

Eighth Act of Grace: Infinite

An act of grace is to know we are infinite with no beginning and no end. A divine spark emerges within the potential of the creator-of-all. Form emerges. That manifestation is bathed in all pervasive grace. If we surrender and accept partnership with the divine, we recognize our place in the whole of creation. We know that we are supported and valued for our contribution not only in our present form but also far beyond. We know we are all one and that the sense of separation or isolation is merely an illusion. We are form within a form organized by grace and expressed as radiant, luminous love. And yet, that form dissolves into an essence held within the infinite organization of grace in relationship with the creator-of-all and divinity. All is perfect, and all is one.

Sometimes infinity and eternity came in a garb to which I
was exquisitely receptive. This was the garb of Grace and
exaltation rather than dread and dislocation. The Grace came
through the song of a bird, wafted in on the scent of a flower
petal, or entered with the rustling of the wind in the trees.

—Sudhir Kakar

I invite you to identify specific outcomes or results of grace in your life and identify and appreciate the laws, states, and acts of grace present in your life. This action will boost your active participation with grace in all aspects of your life.

Now Is the Time to Ask for Grace

Grace is ours for the asking. Why *wouldn't* we ask? We can be ignorant of the fact that we can ask, and can feel unworthy. We might not believe in grace. We may feel we need to earn or merit grace. We may not ask when we realize that our motives are not altruistic but selfish, and we are not willing to face the consequences of those thoughts or actions. We might prefer to remain on the wheel of karma. Perhaps we do not ask because we are tied to the victim role.

Why *would* we ask to live a grace-filled life? We prefer to live life from a position of love, not fear. We desire the twelve states and the eight acts of grace to be constantly present in our daily lives. We prefer a life view of unity, where the connections and interweaving of life events are recognized.

My mother, father, and brother, 1944

My life on the prairies of South Dakota, 1954

CHAPTER 5

• • • • • • • • • • • • • • • • • • • •

My Life Stories

*T*o bring vivid examples of the laws, states and acts of grace, I offer stories from my life, as that is what I know best. It is my desire that you review your life stories, identifying the expressions and results of grace in your life. With recognition and conscious invoking of grace, we surely will choose a life view of unity where all are valued and loved.

> I do not at all understand the mystery of grace—only that it meets us where we are but does not leave us where it found us.

> —Annie Lamott

Awakening and Adjusting—Birth to Eighteen Years of Age

In retrospect, I declare my birth and circumstances surrounding it as an act of grace. I know little of my history except that my biological mother was an unmarried fifteen-year-old high school student of Christian faith and from a small northern plains town. Obviously within her family structure, the decision was made to continue the pregnancy and give me up for adoption.

I was born in the eastern South Dakota town of Aberdeen on December 12, 1938, in a hospital with a local doctor in attendance. In those days, the birth mother was not allowed to see or hold the baby. I was whisked off to the nursery and hidden from view. The same doctor who delivered me knew my adoptive parents were praying for a baby to adopt. Dr. King called my soon-to-be parents, informed them I had been born a day earlier, and asked if they wanted to adopt a healthy seven-pound-ten-ounce newborn baby girl. They said "Yes!" without hesitation.

When I was just three days old, I was taken from that hospital nursery and delivered three blocks away into the outstretched arms of my new mother and father. Although my parents told me I was adopted as soon as I was old enough to understand, my adoptive parents were the only ones with whom I bonded.

From the time I could contemplate my birth, I have accepted the concept that my biological mother's role was to give me physical form and release me. To this day I have no knowledge of the meaning of my birth for my biological mother. We have never met. I am at peace with that fact and know I had the mother that was best for me. Whenever I was asked, "Do you want to know of your biological mother?" I would always reply, "One mother is enough!"

My biological mother expressed several states and acts of grace in her conception and the releasing of me to my adoptive parents. She manifested the divine in birthing a radiant new soul within my physical being. She and her family were clear and committed to releasing me to my new family.

Another outcome of grace so powerfully illustrated in this birth time is that of synchronicity. Dr. King had two unrelated patients—a young girl giving birth and a couple ready to adopt a baby. This happened before agencies were in place with regulations for such transactions. My adoptive parents had similar cultural and religious values and lived in the same physical locale as my biological mother. Dr. King was the pivotal person with the power and the love to facilitate my passage from my biological mother to my adoptive parents.

Since my biological mother was fifteen and unwed when I was born, I believe her pregnancy must have been a traumatic event for her as well as for any of her family members who knew about the pregnancy. They must have offered support, since she wasn't forced to marry the father, and she did choose to give birth to me. By giving me up or releasing me, she gave me a freedom I did not fully realize until some thirty years later.

My adoptive parents were in their early thirties, and in 1938 that was "old" for starting a family. I never knew the reason they could not have their own biological children. Pregnancy and sex were two of many secrets, taboos, and topics that were not discussed in those years.

Fourteen months after my birth, a baby boy was given to my parents by the same doctor. We were reared by the same parents under the same circumstances. As we remember and relate childhood stories today, our experiences are worlds apart in interpretation. If I hadn't shared his home and daily life, I would think we had lived in a different community with different parents under different circumstances!

Perhaps one explanation is that even at an early age, I had felt that I had to take care of myself and not count on others. My brother did not have that same attitude. His expectations differed greatly from mine, and our stories of such memories describe quite different expressions of support and nonsupport. My brother felt he was entitled to pursue activities such as hunting, sports, and playing the guitar.

Furthermore, he expected our parents were to supply the materials, money, training, and transportation so he could participate. He was disgruntled if any of the needed support was not forthcoming on his terms. I also took part in many of the same activities, but usually felt surprise that our parents were there with support. I felt that I had to gather what I needed by myself. Asking for help was most difficult for me. This sibling experience continues to be a potent lesson for me on the power of perception and interpretation.

My father was drafted into World War II at thirty-seven years of age. I was only five at the time. My mother, brother, and I went to live on our maternal grandparents' farm for the two years Father served in the navy. Besides leaving his young family, my father had to give up both his established business of owning and running a service station for vehicles and any income except for his pay as a sailor.

After my father returned from serving in World War II, we moved to the small South Dakota town of Dupree on a Lakota reservation for my early school years from first to twelfth grade. My parents ran a general store and trading post. At first they only sold groceries, but then added clothing, appliances, windmills, and many other items people needed to survive on the prairies of South Dakota.

This little town of 250 people was the only incorporated community on the Cheyenne River Sioux Indian Reservation. Many customers came to town in wagons pulled by horses. My parents accommodated customers day or night. The customers bartered for needed goods or those who were accountable carried a running charge account. I learned not to evaluate others by their skin color or their financial circumstances, but by their honesty and commitment to their agreements.

My father had many roles and tireless energy for service. My father was altruistic. He was the mayor, seeing that the townspeople dug a water well and that the main street received a coat of asphalt to help prevent gumbo soil buildup on wagon and car wheels. He was a volunteer firefighter and the contact for government support for the crippled children association. He donated to the fund-raisers of almost every organization in town. Father was scoutmaster, 4-H leader, and events driver, and he attended my basketball games and concerts and went to 4-H county and state fairs. He always made sure I had horses to ride or a car to drive. My father was a quiet, gentle man who thrived on my joys. He asked nothing more than to visit with the store's customers and to support our small family, financially and emotionally.

My mother was a tall, statuesque woman who bore herself with dignity. She was the creative and steadfast buyer, saleswoman, and bookkeeper for the business. Ranchers came from a hundred miles around to purchase dry goods, notions, clothes, and linens.

Mother insisted on quality. For example, she bought only real glass beads for the American Indian women. She wore and sold elegant hats in this prairie community.

All the family gathered to eat mostly home-cooked meals, plus we had access to a running charge account at the cafe next door. Our stomachs were always filled with quality nutrition. I attribute much of my lifelong, ongoing good health of body and mind to the natural meals, fresh air, and the community watchfulness of my childhood. In our community of 250 people, we truly had a village raising the children. Community residents knew us by name, knew who belonged to whom, and watched over each of us as if we were their own children.

I remember many a night when Mother would say, "I can't talk to you now. I have talked all day." Each night, though, no matter how exhausted she was, Mother would play the same song, dedicated to her father and my grandfather. She had bought the piano with money she received after her father's death. As I listened I would always feel an outpouring of love from my mother and from my grandfather beyond form.

My mother expected excellence in all that my brother and I did. I could have a new dress for the Saturday night dance if I sewed it that week, and the stitching was done correctly. The materials were free and were gotten from the store. Now if I wanted a ready-made dress, I could have that. But I had to pay the wholesale price. That arrangement did encourage me to develop my skills as a seamstress.

I always had the feeling that my mother had a full life but not a fulfilling life. She was not doing what her heart desired. She made her choices and accepted with graciousness the circumstances of her life. I believe she would have preferred a contemplative life with abundant time to pray and be in nature. Mother did find time to grow roses, which elevated her spirit. Roses offered my mother beauty and harmony in her demanding life.

From the time I was seven years old until I turned eighteen, I spent nearly all my time outdoors. I was either riding my horse or my bicycle, exploring the creeks, wading in the cattle dams, or simply walking about our town. I remember feeling content. Nature, even though sometimes harsh, was my most constant companion. The wind would consistently blow from sunup to sundown. It often determined which direction I walked or biked.

On the prairies of South Dakota, I remember the color green as always being treasured and exclaimed over. Another image that remains crisp in my memory is the golden time of sunset when the prairie grasses glowed with radiance. This radiance never failed to make me pause in wonder and appreciation. Whenever I return to the prairie, I am once again in awe of this radiance.

The vivid sounds of childhood are still part of my night dreams and part of my treasured visits back to the Black Hills. I hear the song of the meadowlark on the prairie and the whistling of the wind through the pine trees. I even recall buzzing of flies and mosquitoes omnipresent whether inside or outdoors.

We lived in a comfortable home above our store, and I was required by my loving parents to help in our general store. But mainly I was allowed to roam with freedom, since I was trusted to make good decisions. And for the most part, I did not disappoint my parents. There was no need to be devious or lie, as rules were few, and a minimum number of questions were asked. I find it surprising how little weighing of choices there actually was. Life and activity flowed without much questioning. I was not conflicted or concerned about many issues.

I do know that having a brother who was only fourteen months younger gave me freedom from parental rules since we were mostly out and about together. We were expected to protect and correct each other if necessary. Our parents were wise in that they asked us to share equally in jobs about the home without reference to boy's or girl's work. I grew up with a minimum of sexual stereotypes. Each of us as early as age nine was given the responsibility of managing our time and spending money, and of doing many activities independently.

From an early age, I knew I was intelligent, strong, capable, a leader, and responsible for the outcomes of my actions. I did protect and collaborate with my brother when we pushed the boundaries established for our behaviors. Those rules or boundaries consisted mainly of who we could choose as friends, what time we needed to be in at night, and making sure we completed our chores in an acceptable manner.

The states and acts of grace that I experienced during this early time of awaking and adjusting were the freedom of activity and of time, since my parents had a business to run six days a week. Safety and trust were afforded by the small community and my common sense. My enculturation process was balanced by immersion in the white and Indian ways of knowing. I was indoctrinated with both the spirituality of Christianity and of the Native American culture.

My parents were devoted Roman Catholics in the deepest sense of the word. Not only did they attend devotions and Mass, but they honored the divine in each person they encountered through respect and service. I recall only one expression of negative feelings toward a citizen of our community. The reasons were never discussed with us children. And I am sure my parents prayed for that citizen!

Prayer has always been a part of my daily life, beginning with the morning offering of all my good thoughts, words, and actions, and ending the day with the prayer of gratitude for life and blessings. My earliest recollection is that of praying for grace to guide and support my thoughts and actions. At that time, grace was a concept consistently referred to in the Catholic faith. As a youngster, I had little understanding of it, but I knew it was important and powerful. To know of the existence of grace was such a gift to be given so early in life. I knew I could always call upon grace for support and power. I was also taught within the Catholic doctrine that grace was more tangible for those who embraced certain rituals such as the sacraments and the rituals of passage required to take part in those sacraments. Those sacraments and rituals of passage gave me structure in my early spiritual development.

At the same time, I took part in the native rituals of passage with my Native American friends and the Lakota elders, such as naming ceremonies, vision quests, and releasing of the spirit following physical death. I accepted the grace and blessings available during such powerful ceremonies. I adopted my Native American friend's love of the outdoors. Nature, full of spirits and life, was my early teacher and companion. I prayed and gave thanks to *Tunkashila*, the Creator, and to Jesus Christ, the Way Shower.

When I made my decisions as a young person, I found that there were mainly areas of gray, not black and white. I definitely knew what was right, but not because an outside source said it was so. I was internally guided and confident within myself. At times I conveniently used rules already in place to justify my reasoning. One such rule was, "No sex before marriage because it is a sin." In my reality that was an easy rule, since sex was not a driving need for my well-being as a teenager. Throughout my life I have definitely committed "sins" as defined by man-made doctrines, knowing that the actions I took were right for me and for my development. True discernment, or clarity, is a state of grace that can begin early in life with openness to experience and interpretation.

I had known since elementary school, that I was drawn to the health field as a career. A particular gift of grace that manifested for me was from my high school science teacher, Ms. Bachus. She helped instill in me a love of science and encouraged me to have an inquisitive mind. Her encouragement gave me direction and confidence in my future careers.

In the era when women became nurses, that was my goal. To accomplish that goal, I spent my sophomore year attending a boarding school hundreds of miles from my home to learn Latin and the discipline of mathematics. Naturally, I learned a lot more being with teenage girls with a variety of experiences different from my own.

One experience was treasured then and still recurs in my dreams. The location of the high school was a convent of Presentation Nuns.

Each morning I could go early to Mass and listen to Gregorian chants sung in Latin. If I chose to participate, being nourished with the sound and verse of those chants was a daily gift. At some level I knew the value of those chants and the call to prayer observed by the nuns and students at appointed times each day. Personally, I did not have a religious calling, but to this day I continue to identify those activities and attitudes as an ongoing part of my life.

I completed the courses I needed in one year and thankfully returned to my family and the simple, predictable rural life on the reservation until I graduated from high school. Little did I know that within two years the predictability and ease of my life would change dramatically and that I would embark upon a life path that I had never even thought of or envisioned.

In the following chapters, I continue to relate to those occasions of grace in my personal life that I recognized at the time or later as I would recall the story. May they serve as a stimulus to first recognize grace in your life and next to create a grace-filled life for yourself.

Wedding day, August 23, 1959

Now an RN with full cap strip and pin, 1962

Our family at home, 1978

CHAPTER 6

• • • • • • • • • • • • • • • • • • •

Accepting Responsibility as an Adult

Ages Nineteen to Forty

The winds of Grace blow all the time. All
we need to do is set our sails.

—Ramakrishna

*A*s *I remember leaving my* reservation home at the age of eighteen, I continue to recall specific times in this lifetime when grace supported my actions. Even as a young woman, I recognized the specialness of specific happenings and knew I was experiencing a life filled with excitement, joy and ease. I usually felt "on top of the world." If things were not going in the direction I preferred, I acted to create an acceptable direction. I could be disappointed, sad, or angry at circumstances, but my approach was to rationalize a more positive reason and move on.

Never wavering from the goal of becoming a registered nurse, I was accepted at a diploma school of nursing. This program was run by the same Order of Presentation Nuns I had come to know during my sophomore year of high school. Thus, chanting and prayer were once again at the forefront of daily living. Taking classes and learning, enjoying dormitory life and my social life all flowed.

I could learn easily in the traditional classroom. I heard, I memorized understanding the concept, I regurgitated for tests, and I successfully applied the skills. As student nurses, we used each other as pincushions to practice giving injections and starting IVs. We practiced moving the patient, bathing, and catheterizing with dummies before actually using our new-found skills on patients.

I enjoyed more freedom than usual in a fairly rigid educational and living environment. I was told I was a "favored student" by a couple of the supervising nuns and by several of my friends. I'm not sure why I was favored. A bit of the reason became apparent during my senior year of nursing when I announced to the director, Sister Bernard, that I was going to marry and would be transferring to another school. This nursing program would not allow married women, since marriage was a distraction, and I could well be a "poor influence on the single students." Sister Bernard was angry and shouted, "Someone with your IQ should know better."

Two particular gifts were offered me by individual nuns that have influenced my life ever since that time. As a class, we student nurses were formally taught to meditate. We were asked to close our eyes, picture a black screen, and allow a red rose to fully develop on that screen. That suggestion and permission set a path of contemplative behavior I have faithfully followed to this day. I am receptive to insights and ask for clarity daily.

The second gift came when I was treating a young terminally ill cancer patient. During the day I had administered an intramuscular injection to the thirty-two-year-old woman. She had failed in a suicide attempt made because she was experiencing excruciating pain as the result of a cancer-riddled body. Her two young children and husband stood helplessly by her bedside day after day just waiting for her death and release from the suffering.

That night I lay in my dormitory bed so concerned that I may have caused her extra pain, as the muscle into which I injected the medication was almost nonexistent. Because I was traumatized, I got up and went to the hospital to sit by her bedside near midnight. As I sat by her, an elderly, hunched-over nun in the depth of night came to the bedside and whispered into my ear, "Tell her to look for the light, honey." This saintly nun gave me a tool to lighten my burden of concern. It was a tool I could offer in the future to the many people I was privileged to attend near or at their passing. "Look for the light."

Student nurses complete a psychiatric rotation, and mine was at the state mental hospital. The psych affiliation was a relief from the long hours and constant demands of bedside nursing in the hospital setting. Our schedule was 8:00 a.m. to 5:00 p.m. with only a few night shifts. We came to this rotation to learn, to relax, and even to play.

One of the first nights on campus was a get-acquainted dance that I attended. As fate would have it, or, I should say, as Synchronicity would have it, Ken, a senior at the local college, needed a date for the next night and came to the dance with that goal. Ken was also living at the state mental hospital, where he worked nights as an orderly on the men's violent ward to assist with his educational expenses. Since he was on the state hospital campus, he could attend the activities of student nurses.

Ken tells the story that he walked into the room where the dance was being held, saw me, and had a brief vision of him and me wearing tunics by a well. He was my younger brother in that scene. Ken said he knew instantly I was the person he was going to marry. This is such a vivid example of the act of grace that I call dimensionality.

While we were dancing, Ken asked me to go out with him and two friends for a steak dinner the next night, and I said yes. Steaks at a sit-down restaurant surely beat institutional food in the hospital cafeteria.

We were inseparable for the next six weeks except for school, work, and a little sleep. When Ken graduated from college, I met his parents when they arrived from Chicago to celebrate. Ken's mom, Margaret, must have seen more seriousness in the relationship than Ken and I were admitting. Margaret made me cook bacon and eggs for breakfast in the kitchenette of their motel room. I had to laugh at the oddity of such a request and her not-so-subtle checking out of my cooking skills. Seeing the humor of the situation eliminated any possible feelings of trepidation or being put upon. And I guess I passed!

Ken had signed a teaching contract in California and felt obligated to honor it now that he had graduated. I had a year left of schooling to become a registered nurse. We each had a career plan, and they did not include being together. Our individual lives were full, and we were sailing along. Ken left for California and summer classes at Redlands University as he had planned. I finished the psychiatric affiliation, continuing to work and enjoy recreation with friends.

I had two weeks at home before going on to the next rotation of pediatrics. Ken and I were talking on the telephone daily and exchanging letters. It became obvious we wanted to be together. But it was the late fifties, and given our strict family values, we didn't even consider living together before marriage.

Separation was intolerable, and without much further discussion or planning we simply decided during one phone conversation to get married. The only stipulation was that Ken would find a school of nursing into which I could transfer my credits. He did that within the week. How amazing! We were together six weeks. We were separated for two weeks, and within two more weeks we had decided to marry. Of course, the nuns at my school of nursing were upset with my marrying someone I had just met. They were upset as well that I was leaving for California. But I never questioned that all was in order, and we were doing exactly what was right for us. That clarity is the result of living in grace.

Although my parents still had not met Ken, my mother said, "You have always made good decisions, and we trust you are making a good decision now." Ken returned to South Dakota a week before the wedding and met both my immediate and my extended family of grandparents, aunts, uncles, and cousins. We were married with both our families and our friends in attendance and left for California that night right after the wedding. I was twenty years old and leaping into this new life with my new husband, and without any doubt.

Our all-knowing beginning has continued for fifty-plus years. Ken still recalls the dress I was wearing that fateful night we met, and we literally give thanks each day for the pure love and joy this union brings us.

Our honeymoon consisted of moving to California, halfway across the country, and beginning our life together. I experienced a sadness leaving my family and town behind but did not question my decision or dwell on that loss. Ken and I felt a profound love, respect, and trust for each other and for whatever was to come. A smile that extended to our souls was ever-present, and we constantly told each other how blessed we were. Early on we knew we deserved this lifetime of love, joy, and ease.

From the very beginning of our life together, we did not plan details of how our lives and work would unfold. Ken honored his commitment to teaching junior high students, and I continued my nursing education. Within three years, we had two young sons, and I had my RN degree.

The concept of abundance was our umbrella, and we had the energy and resources to take full advantage of the diversity of culture and activities offered in the state of California. We traveled to the beach cities, the mountain towns, and the desert lands. Like many new families, during the week before payday we often searched through pockets for milk money. I remember being physically tired, but I do not recall being worried about circumstances or what might be next. We had each other and trusted all was in perfect order if we did our part.

As a take-charge woman with definite ideas of the qualities I wanted in my life, I knew our children would be delivered naturally without drugs in their systems. In the early sixties, mechanical medicine was entrenched to the point where the mother-to-be was anesthetized, the father was banished to the waiting room, and breast feeding was frowned upon after the baby arrived.

There is no other way to explain it, but we were living supported by the laws of grace. I knew what I wanted, I set the intention and would settle for nothing less. With trust and prayer, I was guided to Dr. Evarts Loomis in the neighboring town. Evarts Loomis, MD, was a renowned homeopathic physician who had established a Whole Person Health Program and promoted natural childbirth, whole foods, and breast feeding the newborns. Dr. Loomis helped deliver our first two sons using natural childbirth techniques. Dr. Loomis went on to be the cofounder of the American Holistic Medical Association. I was recently gifted two of his books that I plan to pass on to the sons he helped enter this world.

Three years in California was enough, and we packed our car to return to South Dakota, as extended family was a priority. We were now a family of four, and we wanted grandparents to be an influence in the lives of our little ones. Baby things increased our load, but Ken was an efficient packer. We loaded all our belongings and moved in our station wagon. This was before infant car seats, so space was more flexible.

The town of Eagle Butte, South Dakota, next to my early home of Dupree, had been established as tribal headquarters. We discovered that a new boarding and community school had been created to serve Indian students from the reservation as well as local non-Indian students. Ken was hired as the high school communication teacher, and we moved into a government-subsidized duplex twenty miles from my parents' home and store. This represented our first return to the Cheyenne River Sioux Indian Reservation.

Life was full with new friends, school activities, and coping with the harsh prairie summers and winters. Our third son and our only daughter arrived during the four years we lived in Eagle Butte. Since we were non-Indians, we could not use the Indian Health Service Hospital. That meant traveling two hundred miles to a hospital to deliver our number three son and 150 miles to another hospital for our daughter.

I was so thankful that I was a nurse, and we prepared for many eventualities. An example of the power of clarity of intention occurred during the long trip to the hospital for the birth of our son, Michael. My contractions were fast and furious as we arrived, midpoint in our trip, at the only town with a hospital.

We needed to stop or risk an uncomfortable car delivery. The doctor was dictatorial and said he would manage the delivery according to his terms, not my desires. Furthermore, the delivery was imminent. With this proclamation from the doctor, my labor ceased, and within a few hours I was released to return home. The following night we successfully drove the full two hundred miles as we had originally planned. In hindsight I could have stayed home and delivered our little ones, but I was steeped in the need for medical intervention if necessary. I was not willing to take such a risk.

We found a woman who was able to care for four little ones two and a half days a week, and I went to work as a clinic nurse for Indian Health Service. A licensed practical nurse, a medical doctor, and I would travel up to a hundred miles each way to outlying clinics to administer to people near their homes. I gained such respect and empathy with the Indian people sharing our lives together in this personal way. We cooperated with the local elders and medicine people to foster compliance with health and medical practices. I recognized a general distrust of non-Indian personnel telling local residents what they should do. That distrust had been earned over the years. For example, on this reservation US soldiers had presented tribal members with blankets infested with the small pox virus to eliminate many of the Native population. Alcohol was also introduced, and continues to the present time to be destructive to the Native person's body and spirit. Drugs and experiments were fostered on the Native populations, usually followed by unfulfilled promises and treaties.

However, our team had some advantages for building trust. The licensed practical nurse was a local tribal member, and the elders remembered me as a youngster at the store where my parents offered goods to them and their families. Furthermore, the medical doctor was reserved and respectful. In this isolated town of Eagle Butte, with three hundred people, I was given the opportunity to use my nursing skills, to learn more deeply Native American ways, and to be a salaried member of a professional team.

Now, I was a daughter, a wife, a mother, and a professional. During this time of my life, I truly perfected the skills of balancing and surrendering the details within the larger picture. Praying for guidance, wisdom, and love to accomplish what I had taken on, I gave thanks each night for receiving a daily outpouring of the love, joy, and abundance.

I am sure there were times when I questioned if I really could do all that I had set in motion. My memory is selective, and I only recall now the fun we had with our children, my parents, and our friends.

However, I do recall the harsh realities of living on the South Dakota prairies. During one winter blizzard in the early sixties, the snow blew horizontally, entirely covering the windows layer by layer. If we could have gone outside, it would have been an easy walk onto the roof. Then the wind shifted, and the drifts were completely blown to another location. The ground was left bare. All was well inside our home as the electricity stayed on for heat, light, and cooking. After a few days the wind subsided, and the blizzard finally receded. The remaining drifts left in place were often twenty feet high. Aquifers were filled, but lives were lost. Our neighbor Harold was driving with two passengers on the two-lane hard-surface road between Ridgeview and Eagle Butte. Their car stalled. When the wind ceased a day later, and the snowplows could safely be out on the roads, the three men were found in the car, frozen to death. Near the car, in a corner of the field, over two dozen cows were crowded together, all frozen where they stood.

Our next adventure would take us from those frozen prairies to the humid warmth of the South. Ken, who is an excellent writer, applied for and received a grant from the National Science Foundation. This grant offered our family of six the opportunity to move from Eagle Butte to the University of Florida, in Gainesville.

While there, Ken completed his master's degree in guidance and counseling. Talk about abundance! We received more income from the grant than from our combined salaries of teaching and nursing in South Dakota. We lived in Florida the year that desegregation was mandated. We observed up close the prejudice and the change of perception that desegregation required. The difference in southern culture was emphasized by the food provided when our fifth child was born in a local hospital. It was New Year's Eve, and I was served black-eyed peas and hog jowls.

Our life was expanding. We now had five children, with the oldest in first grade. We trusted we were in synchronicity with our passions and purposes, not knowing where we would be next or what we would be doing. We appreciated how supported we were with income, friends, and experiences. It was with great ease that we enjoyed the southern beauty and learned about the flora and fauna of the swamps and bayous.

We definitely had much to learn about mildew, mold, fungi, coral snakes, and alligators. It rained nearly every afternoon. We would hang our damp jackets in the closet, and by the next day mildew had spread to the surrounding jackets. This never happened in South Dakota.

Occasionally we would ask what our five- and six-year-old sons had done on their way home from school. They would announce that they had thrown stones at the alligator in the pond between school and home! These experiences were part of our daily lives, and at times it felt as if we were on another planet.

One significant story of our year and a half in Florida illustrates the presence of grace in our lives. We rented a rural home, and Ken traveled to the university some days with a friend. Our house had central heat, which consisted of a kerosene-fueled stove in the center of the home encased with drywall on three sides. One day the stove continued to heat, drawing in more fuel even though I had turned the rheostat to off. The wall was hot to the touch, and the stove was turning red hot. I got the children outside and called the university for Ken. Meanwhile Ken perceived my need and danger. Ken had no explanation of how he knew there was a major problem at home; he just knew. He asked the friend for his car keys and was on his way out of the building when the message reached him.

My explanation is that dimensional communication was possible because of our love, Ken's receptivity, and the outpouring of the presence of grace in our lives. All life is truly organized to be of benefit when we recognize and invoke grace. Ken drove home with urgency. He listened to my story of the red-hot stove and immediately shut off the fuel at its source at the tank behind our house. He learned of this in tents in cold Korea, where the stoves tended to overheat. We both marveled at how the need was communicated with ease and clarity, and action was taken with trust, not panic, but with urgency.

Our two sons' asthma, aggravated by the molds and fungi, was so challenging that it became obvious we needed to leave Florida. So the day Ken graduated with his master's degree in counseling, we packed our belongings into the station wagon and the four-by-six rental trailer, which we could pull. We drove out of Florida trusting that our next destination and work would become known. We knew that what was to be next would become clear if we paid attention to synchronistic events and signs. We appreciated the freedom offered by no schedule, no timelines, and no set destination. The seven of us traveled north and west as a self-contained unit of joy and love within a benevolent universe.

We stopped in Chicago at the home of Ken's parents. We came to realize how important it was to see Ken's parents and to have a respite from travel. It seemed right, as well, to spend time with my parents back in South Dakota. On the way, we traveled slowly, stopping to play in parks, eat, swim, and sleep in motels. Our daily life was a simple vacation with no timelines or demands, and we were not concerned with what was next. We really didn't need to know yet. It was summer in the Midwest, and all was well.

We arrived back in my hometown of Dupree on the Indian reservation where my parents still operated the general store. My parents took us in with such pure love and joy. The children began a lifelong bonding with their grandparents.

As the time was approaching for school to begin for our sons who were going into first and second grade, Ken and I considered where we would like to put down roots. I shared with Ken that when I was a youngster I would declare, "When I get big I am going to live in the Black Hills, and specifically in Spearfish." Reading a regional newspaper, Ken saw an advertisement for a counseling position on the Pine Ridge Reservation that involved a traveling unit based in Rapid City in the Black Hills. The position required a doctorate degree. Ken had just received a master's degree, but he had experience working on a reservation. Ken applied for the position. Since he clearly had the skill required, he was hired. We were on our way to live in the Black Hills of South Dakota within the week.

Three memorable happenings that impacted our lives occurred during the four years we lived in Rapid City. First, we bought our first home, and that meant we began to accumulate furniture and "stuff." I wondered if we would ever be able to move just using our car again. A time would come when we would discover that answer.

The second happening was the entrance of Felice Leonardo Buscaglia into our lives in the late sixties. In a dimensional act of grace, Ken met Leo walking down the hall in the Rapid City Howard

Johnson motel. They both had instant recognition of their connection, and Ken invited Leo home to dinner. Thus began an earthly love affair that lasted until Leo passed some thirty-plus years later.

Leo Buscaglia, PhD, was a professor at the University of Southern California in the Special Education Department. He and Ken were both dedicated to improving educational possibilities for all children. Leo went on to publish numerous books. Three of Leo's books on the *New York Times* bestseller list were: *Love, Personhood,* and *Living, Loving and Learning.* Dr. Buscaglia influenced the lives of many across the world with his books, published in eight languages, and with his public broadcasting and personal appearances. And he became my personal mentor.

A third memorable event served as an outpouring of grace in strengthening family ties and the creation of loving memories. Surrounded with the beauty and opportunities of the Black Hills, we decided to select a family-oriented long-term activity for winter. Our choices were narrowed to snowmobiling, cross-country skiing, and downhill skiing. We decided on downhill skiing.

Skiing was a constant in our family life for a good twenty years. Not only did we ski weekly on local slopes, but we also ventured to the Rocky Mountain slopes across four states during yearly vacations. Our ski equipment was safe even though it consisted of hand-me-downs. We carried our meals in brown bags and coolers. When our friends asked other friends if the slopes were crowded, the answer was, "Yes, the Engelhardts were there!"

Skiing with the entire family was a priority that demanded time, resources, and commitment. In return, we were offered such sharing of love, joy, and beauty. Family cooperation, responsibility, and communication were demanded for this activity to be safe and fun. Who would have known a simple choice of a family winter sport would lead to the development of lifestyle values and lifelong memories?

During these busy years, it never occurred to me to search for or to know more about my birth mother. My life was full and happy. But there came a time when I had two reasons to seek more information. First, I needed my exact time of birth for an astrological chart. Secondly, I became interested in health history for my children as well as for myself.

So when I was twenty-eight years old, I traveled to the South Dakota State Capitol building in Pierre. I approached a clerk in a basement office of the building to check on my birth certificate. She informed me that I would need a court order to see my original certificate.

Then she asked me an astonishing question, "What was your maiden name?" When I told her, the woman said, "I remember you and your biological mother and grandmother." It was indeed an act of grace for that woman to be in that office at that time. The synchronicity of the two of us coming together that day provided my children and me with meaningful information. The woman went on to say that she probably knew where the biological family still lived. She told me if I wanted to write a letter and ask any questions, she would do her best to get the letter to them.

I did write the letter and asked many questions. And with clarity I also told my biological mother that I was happy and that my life was good. Within two weeks I had a response from my birth mother by way of the clerk at the capitol with my time of birth. Although I had not asked, she gave me information about my biological father. My father was seventeen when I was born. He had joined the navy and was later lost at sea. That was the extent of her knowledge.

What was significant in her response was that she had married, and her husband knew of my existence. However, none of her three other children had been told about me. I clearly knew then that there would be no further contact. That was all right with me. I already had a mother and really did not feel the need for another.

Shortly after this communication with my biological mother, I fully came to know the freedom she had given me when she released me to my parents. In my early thirties, I had the opportunity to attend the Creative Problem Solving Institute in New York State. I chose to attend a session facilitated by a friend of mine. I wanted to support her by my presence and participation. Little did I know what a revealing session it would turn out to be.

The experience was for five of us to form a circle around a person in the center and orchestrate movements based on a word given us by the facilitator that we shouted or whispered to the center person. These words could be spoken all at once or called out individually. Background music that varied in tempo and rhythm helped orchestrate that person's movements as well. When it was my turn in the center, one of the words given by the facilitator to a circle person was "abandonment." That was the word I heard most vividly over and over. I found myself crouching and finally lying barely moving in the fetal position on the floor. I felt profound sadness. Then suddenly, in the next instant, I found myself rising up. I flung open my arms. My heart was opened, and I danced with full abandon. In those few minutes I truly experienced both sides of the same coin—the restriction of feeling "abandoned" and at the same time, the freedom of living with "abandon." I also realized that this amazing gift of freedom was given to me by my biological mother. I shared my story with the other participants in my circle and told of the gratitude I felt for her act of giving me to my parents.

During this span of time, Ken's counseling work on the Pine

Ridge Indian Reservation was so effective that he was asked to be the director of an American Indian-focused Teacher Corps. It was a federal program based at Black Hills State College in Spearfish, South Dakota. My childhood intention of living in the beauty of Spearfish in the Black Hills now manifested with ease.

My parents continued their outpouring of trust and pure love, and loaned us money to buy land and build our dream home. We chose three acres of land on a spring-fed creek with a small homestead house and barn. The owner had built a new home across the creek, which later was purchased by my parents when they left their business and the reservation.

We designed our home for the seven of us, and I was the general contractor. We hired a father and his three sons to do most of the building. They guided me to the best subcontractors. During the eight months of construction, we led a simple life in the homestead cabin, sleeping seven abreast in sleeping bags across the room.

Without knowing the full implications, we decided upon an octagonal living room holding the center of all the living spaces in our new home. Little did we know what the full implications of that decision would be! The magic experienced by family and friends coming together in this eight-sided room is best explained by two ancient symbols. This eight-sided geometrical shape is an ancient symbol for the Great Mother Goddess as Nourisher. This nourishing Great Mother is likewise depicted as the eight-legged spider of Grandmother Spider in Native American mythology. The spider is the weaver. Grandmother Spider weaves the threads that hold the patterns set forth in family life. These transformations were set into motion for our families and all who entered that octagonal living room. For the twenty years we were in this home, we hosted multiple family holiday gatherings there that established traditions, held parties for adults and for children, and gatherings for spiritual questioning and growth. This eight-sided room nurtured the minds and souls of those who entered.

The home, our children, and our social life were primarily my responsibility for the next few years. Ken was involved in guiding the educational program of American Indian students across seven South Dakota reservations receiving their bachelor of arts and later their master's degrees. These native students lived and worked on their home reservations and only came to the university campus during summer weeks. Many of these nontraditional students would later come to be local and national educational leaders. Ken was recognized for his leadership and creativity in designing these programs and for guiding them through bureaucracies. The synchronicity of the federally funded Teacher Corps program, Ken's clarity as a visionary, and the freedom afforded by being outside the traditional educational system all attested to the presence of grace and Ken's willingness to partner with divinity, the force of love, in his professional life. He traveled continually across the state and nation, as he was appointed to boards and committees, and his professional status soared.

Our home was finished, and daily life was healthy, efficient, and easy. We had raw milk and fresh eggs from local farms, produce from local gardens, meat from local ranchers, cars to drive, and horses to ride. Our youngest child entered school. The bus picked up and delivered our five children to our door each school day even though we lived ten miles out in the country.

I was thirty-two years old. I felt a void, a diminished sense of joy and bliss. I now had several hours a day just for myself. I decided to attend the local university, since that left me in charge of my time and still available for our children. Ken was supportive and truly loved all activities involved with home and family life when he was available.

Majoring in biology with a minor in chemistry, I fed my need to know and be stimulated in the science arena. This was financially possible, since I was a spouse of a university teaching staff member and could attend tuition free. This fact was an act of grace offering me abundance and freedom.

Pursuing this degree offered me a lifeline of challenges, friends, and knowledge, and a sense of new adventures waiting to be manifested in my life. I valued and was reinforced in the image of "wonder woman." However, adding the student role did increase my level of stress, and I began to experience migraine and cluster headaches with increasing frequency. While it appeared I could do it all with competence and ease, the occurrence and pain of headaches told me there was a lack of balance and harmony. Something needed to change.

I did not want to change my roles and lifestyle, so I chose to change my reaction and response to the stress that lifestyle put upon my physical and emotional selves. I would not accept pain beyond its red flag warnings of imbalance and would not accept medication to ameliorate the pain without attending to the cause. That led me to discover how to manage the stress and pain by learning skills that promoted balance and maximized well-being. I turned to what I knew of anatomy, physiology, and chemistry, as well as the latest thoughts and technology in the field of health.

The tools and technology of biofeedback had recently been made available to the general public. Here was a natural way to study and alter body reactions. I rented an electromyograph (EMG), a thermo-feedback instrument sensitive to the nearest one-tenth of a degree, and a brainwave feedback, and training instrument. Using these three instruments, I developed a protocol of feedback and practice. Within a month I could reduce muscle tension and warm my hands at will. My headaches diminished. I was given the freedom to continue my demanding lifestyle pain-free.

In an act of synchronicity, combining my background of scientific inquiry, my success at learning to self-regulate my own physiology, and my need for our children to succeed in their young lives, I was led to develop and implement a program of self-discovery and self-regulation within our public school system.

I became acquainted with a research specialist and met with him about structuring and developing a research model for self-discovery and self-regulation within the public school system. Many years later, I would again be led to this research specialist for another purpose entirely!

With clarity and ease, I was able to set forth a program that involved nine hours of awareness, imagery, and biofeedback practice. These hours were spread out over six weeks. The participants volunteered to be part of the program and ranged in age from six years old to eighty years old. Men, women, and students from kindergarten to twelfth grade learned self-regulation skills to improve performance in their chosen areas, to remediate health problems, or to maintain wellness.

To enhance my credibility within the educational community, I received my bachelor's degree in education and was hired by the school system as a teacher. Students and teachers completed the self-regulation program in the classrooms during the school day, and parents and community members participated in the evenings.

We found significant educational and statistical results in the measured areas of self-concept and general anxiety reduction. General anxiety is that sense of anxiousness and tension that is not attached to a specific cause or situation. Hundreds of participants learned to regulate muscle tension and control hand temperature at will, thus improving the health results and performance standards they sought.

Since the program was proven to be educationally and statistically significant, it was accepted for national distribution. This single three-year study catapulted me into consulting across the nation. I published an instruction manual and two student handbooks to help other schools adopt this self-regulation program as part of their curriculum.

Such joy and abundance of recognition and appreciation were the results of being aligned with grace. With gratitude I recognized that I was manifesting divinity by acknowledging my personal needs and then finding an avenue to share my knowledge and experience.

I was now thirty-nine years of age, and our five children were all teenagers. My mother-in-law, my parents, and my brother with his family were all living as *tiospayae*, the Lakota word for extended family. Our families were showered with an outpouring of pure love.

But I was not content. There was more to know and more to do. My mentor, Leo Buscaglia, had just returned from being with a teacher in Thailand, and he came to our home for a visit. I asked Leo if he thought I needed to find a spiritual teacher. He looked squarely at me and said, "Loretta, you have everything you need right here." At that point I knew with clarity that I was living within the laws of grace. I no longer questioned my guidance and decisions.

Over the years Leo had encouraged me to obtain my doctorate, especially because of the doors it would open. He further encouraged me to write each day. I admit I did not follow Leo's prompting to do daily writing until much later. In my seventh decade I began writing this book. And even now, I don't write every day.

During a visit to our home in 1978, as we had breakfast, Leo said to me, "I know who is for you." I soon became aware that he meant who was to be my major advisor in my graduate program. Within the hour, Leo was on the telephone to the University of Northern Colorado, setting up an interview with his friend who would guide my graduate work in the field of psychophysiology.

My program of study was soon developed, and an abundance of outstanding scholars and practitioners from the biofeedback and educational world agreed to supervise and sign off on my course work. For two years I was to experience an outpouring of pure love and support as I pursued this degree. Even with the support, I recognized that I was courting transformation and risking what I knew as my comfort zone.

Transformation is energy changing form. I had often offered resistance to that new form, mainly due to fear of the unknown. At times, I had preferred the status quo, even if the old form had outlived its purpose. For example, I had felt the need to take care of myself and not count on others. This attitude was helpful for me as a child and young adult and served me well. I directed my life and accepted responsibility for my decisions.

I didn't recognize the opportunity to share that responsibility and control until eighteen years into my marriage. All along Ken was always steadfast in expressing his love, support, and appreciation for me and for all I did. I heard him but reserved a part of myself that whispered, "You have to do it yourself!" I did not fully trust situations where I didn't feel that I had control of the outcome. I once had a wise woman say to me, "Loretta, you greet everyone on the front steps of your castle, but no one enters." I was surprised since I had felt that I was open and welcoming even to strangers. That message was profound for me. I began to question the isolation implied by that insight. I began to open my castle door a crack and allow a shaft of the golden light of grace to illuminate the interior.

I came to see that it was not a matter of duality with another person being responsible or with me being responsible, but it was a shared responsibility. My either/or duality was transformed with that insight. My visible behavior did not change, and I doubt that Ken could pinpoint the change. What changed was my deep-felt reality. I was not fully responsible, and my world would not collapse if I did not hold it up. With that insight, I experienced such freedom and deepening of love to truly share myself, with all my strengths and weaknesses. I knew I was loved and cherished for just being, not doing.

This transformational insight helped make it possible for me to leave our five teenagers and Ken for two years of graduate school and truly relish a different life form. I was ecstatic at living alone for the first time in my adult life, attending engrossing seminars and interacting with new friends. I did not feel homesick or lonesome and gave full attention to daily life and educational demands.

I did spend time with family about every six weeks when several free days came together. That time was rich and love-filled. Ken and the kids were working together as a well-coordinated unit. I was the valued visitor during those visits. I was proud of them and never felt jealous of the lifestyle they adopted in my absence. Ken summed it up well. He would tell others, "Loretta left and earned a degree, and I stayed home and got an education!"

At forty years of age I returned home, educated and credentialed with what Ken called a "terminal degree," a doctorate in the study of psychophysiology. It was terminal from the viewpoint that surely this was all the formal education I would need to teach, counsel, and develop models of healthy living. The roles of wife, mother, daughter,

daughter-in-law, sister, and aunt were back in place, valued and appreciated. I fully recognized what a freedom and blessing I had been given by my family out of pure love—the act of encouraging me to go and then welcoming me back. My daughter Sharon expressed it succinctly when I was leaving. She said, "It will be hard with all 'guy energy' in the home, but it's important that you do what you have to do."

I never second-guessed my decision to leave. I just enjoyed living alone for the first time in my adult life. I focused on my growth. Now that I had grown personally and professionally, it was time to give back. It was time to be altruistic and put the welfare of others in the forefront once again.

Grand entry at Takini Wacipi

Embroidered jacket with Takini School
logo awarded for years of service.

· · · · · · · · · · · · · · · · · ·

CHAPTER 7

Questioning and Refining

Ages Forty-One to Sixty

*I*n the mid-1980s, Ken had an opportunity to take a sabbatical from the university and pursue his doctorate, four hundred miles across our state. That meant it was time for me to use my educational credentials, experience, and creativity, and be receptive to what my world was about to offer. I trusted in abundance, joy and clarity of purpose in whatever was to be my next endeavor.

Innovative educational grants were available then for successful, creative educational programs targeting public school students, grades one through twelve. Needing to support our family for a couple of years, I secured the position of director of a middle school program involving a caring, empowering disciplinary approach.

There was no doubt that I was functioning within the laws of grace. Such a program supported manifesting the divine, the power of love, within each student, teacher, and parent participating. The disciplinary approach promoted clarity regarding the value of chosen attitudes and behaviors. Students had freedom to choose their behaviors, knowing the consequences beforehand.

The program results were positive, and once again I was consulting with other school personnel who adopted or adapted our program. I submitted a proposal to write and record a telecourse consisting of twelve half-hour sessions to be produced and televised throughout the state's public broadcasting system.

This television endeavor was new to me, but I recognized the opportunity to share ideas that invited clarity, joy, and freedom into the lives of those who were receptive. Both processes—conceptualizing and writing—were intense, but I did trust in the outpouring of grace to accomplish what I had proposed. The telecourse was chosen for national distribution and remained on the air and available for graduate credit from the University of South Dakota for eleven years. This was beyond the copyright permission I had received for a couple of music pieces used in the programming. No one protested. Perhaps it was because of my purity of intent to help develop loving, altruistic young people without having a profit motive.

I was in awe of what had been accomplished with relative ease. It produced a big grin to observe myself on television ten years later or have students approach me and say, "I saw you on TV this morning." It was a good thing I had white hair by the time I was forty years old when we filmed the telecourse, or there would have been a glaring difference for new viewers ten years later.

Over the next seven years, our children left home one by one to pursue their adult lives. Three paid their own way through college with the help of jobs, grants, and scholarships. We experienced much joy as all five children grew into productive, caring adults. We will always be there for them, but our launching responsibility was mainly completed. We continue to be so proud of our four sons and our daughter.

With each new opportunity and endeavor came the inspiration to question and refine my thoughts and behavior. I remembered the wise advice of mentor Leo, "If you ask the correct question, you have the answer." Great care was taken in posing the questions regarding my life purpose and how best to serve and create the ongoing presence of joy and gratitude in my daily life.Our family began to cultivate our next big endeavor. With the input of our five adult children and their four spouses, we created a life and business plan for a family-owned and operated health-centered resort. I assumed the responsibility for creating this plan, as I had the expertise, time, and motivation.

After visiting several states and Costa Rica, we chose Sedona, Arizona, as the location for our resort. I moved to Sedona and positioned myself as a front desk employee at the resort we intended to purchase. This action provided a bottom-up education into resort operation. For the next two years, I walked through every open door to manifest the investor who could see the opportunity offered by our family dream. As I explored Sedona, a friend and I bought and operated a home health care business to provide financial support. However, in a later stage of my life, I would come to realize that operating this business was also preparing me in unexpected ways for yet another adventure.

Our family members possessed degrees in community education, psychophysiology, parks and recreation, psychology/gerontology, business administration, aeronautical engineering, and pharmacy. We had the credentials and expertise to be effective and successful operating a health-centered resort.

Two financing opportunities seemed possible. However—and this is hard for me to admit—it turned out that neither one was viable. One had unacceptable conditions attached to it, and the other one could very well have been a scam.

After a few years, I gave up active pursuit of the resort plan and just surrendered. I had done what I knew to do. It seemed obvious that all was not aligned to manifest our dream in the timeline we set forth. I do still feel a loss of us not being physically together as a *tiospaye*, an extended family. It had been such a joy contemplating all of us—now it would be twelve adults and eleven grandchildren—living and working together. To this day, the resort has not become a reality, but the potential is still alive. We are still in place. We are just older and wiser. But I did not label the effort as a "failure" or blame any circumstance. It felt like the letting go shifted the spotlight of intention to my next experience.

For twenty years our home base had remained in Spearfish on the acreage ten miles from town. One of the joys of living there was that my parents lived just two hundred yards away across Chicken Creek. The creek supported brook trout, and my mother and our son David loved fishing together. They would occasionally fish for our breakfast.

Perhaps that was the introduction of David's lifelong passion for nature and all its beauty. David truly is a "horse whisperer" and to this day follows his passion by living on forty acres along with his family and their three horses. I vividly recall David saying as a young adult, "My idea of worship and where I feel the closest to God is floating on an inner tube and fly fishing on Pactola Lake, surrounded by granite boulders and pine trees." David knows with clarity that nature offers him harmony, the sense of pure love, abundance, and nourishment for body and soul.

Toward the end of those twenty years several synchronistic events resulted within the time span of two years that drastically altered our future. Hindsight shows that the divine was manifesting to open the way for an outpouring of love and freedom in our personal and professional lives. I must say it didn't feel like it at the time, as we had established a narrow, predictable, and comfortable existence.

Both my parents passed on within two years of each other. That profound loss was accompanied with new-found freedom. Ken's mother, who had been with us for ten years, left our home space and moved to a subsidized apartment in town, gaining friends and activities outside the family realm.

New men were hired as university president and vice president where Ken was employed as dean of the continuing education program. The new faculty-members expressed a different philosophy as to the purpose of the outreach for this program. Since their vision was contrary to his, Ken felt he could no longer be employed by that institution. He took early retirement, remaining true to his vision.

Our last anchor was pulled up and, once again, we were ready to sail! We trusted there were infinite possibilities from which to choose our next expression of living life fully. We did let our friends and networks of professionals know we were available. We did not worry or set expectations, just remained receptive to what would manifest. Our responsibility to others was minimal, and we were debt-free. We were in our fifties, and life was simple at this juncture. We were able to ask this question, "In what arena would we next immerse ourselves with passion that would also be altruistic?"

The answer came within two weeks. A Native American friend who had received his master's degree in the Teacher Corps program under Ken's tutelage approached Ken with a need. The most isolated area of his reservation needed a school administrator to help the school survive and prepare for the combining of three community schools into one. Combining the schools had been mandated by the

Bureau of Indian Affairs after the bureau began construction of a new school facility on the prairie in the center of the three communities.

These communities had a reputation of not fully appreciating each other. A strong, visionary leader was needed who also could navigate the political waters of Washington, DC, where funding was appropriated under treaty rights. Ken had firmly established his heartfelt pure love for the Native Lakota people. Now they were inviting him to their land to live and work in a leadership position.

Ken did not hesitate to see the potential and approached me with the idea. I could hardly believe that we were circling back for a third time to the reservation where I grew up. Once we were invited as guests, and the elders discovered that they had known me as a youngster, I knew we were accepted and would not have to go through the rigorous testing of most non-Indian personnel.

My only requirement was that we would have a clean place to live, since the school building was condemned. We found a $4,000 trailer house and had it moved to the reservation. The floor slanted, and the walls vibrated with the prairie wind. But we had a bathroom, running water, and a furnace that worked!

Within the year Ken was asked to be superintendent of the new school. I was asked to be the curriculum specialist and federal compliance officer. We accepted and oversaw the new beginnings of an early childhood through twelfth grade school accredited by both the State of South Dakota and the Bureau of Indian Affairs. The school board voted to contract for full governance of this new school and to be accountable for government funding and program development. Usually this is handled by the Bureau of Indian Affairs. This action gave us local control for budget, management, and visionary decisions.

The full-blooded Lakota people, descendants of the 1890 Wounded Knee Massacre, wanted their school built upon the Lakota values of honesty, respect, generosity, spirituality, courage, and wisdom. The people chose the name Takini School. One interpretation of the Lakota word, *Takini*, is "survivor." The logo of a four-direction medallion with seven eagle feathers was created by a community member. The mascot, a sky hawk, was chosen by the student body and was incorporated into the logo.

The symbolism of this logo and this mascot illustrates the depth of the hopes and traditions of the Lakota people involved in creating Takini School.

The four-direction medallion represents the four directions or, as the Lakota people say, the four winds. The north direction is represented by the color white. It calls forth the wisdom and gratitude as described in the stories of the elders, told especially during the snowy months of winter. Red represents the east and is the place of rumination and clarity. The east wind brings greater understanding of other levels or dimensions of life. Innocence and the energy of the child are found in the south direction. This south wind, represented by the color yellow, allows the trust, the beauty, and the joy of living to be expressed. The Lakota way depicts the west as black. It is the wind of introspection. We are encouraged to enter the dark cave and discover how we can best serve ourselves and all our relations.

The seven eagle feathers grouped below the medallion represent the seven community ceremonies of the Lakota people served by Takini School. These ceremonies maintain the center of traditional teachings and convey the power to understand and connect with the Above Beings for the well-being of all.

Following is a brief overview of deep and meaningful expressions of community practice represented by the seven eagle feathers in the logo of Takini School. The ceremony central to all ceremonies is the sun dance, *Wiwangwacipi*. It is held in a large open circle at the height of the summer when the sun is at full strength. The participants dance around a sacred tree called the sun pole placed in the center of the circle. The dancers pledge their efforts for all the tribe, and the four days of dancing is the rite of rebirth, renewal, new life, and thanksgiving. This ceremony was not held at the school, but nearby at two different reservations.

The other six central ceremonies were held at Takini School or in nearby communities. The sweat lodge, *Inipi*, was held often when the need was perceived for purification or purging of negative energy, for healing, and for prayers for specific concerns brought forth by students, staff, or community members.

The *Yuwipi* ceremony is performed by a medicine man for healing, for seeking answers to questions, and for finding lost articles.

Puberty rites, *Isnati Ca Ltnvan* or song of isolation, are for young women. This ceremony involved the teaching of social responsibility of Lakota women.

The sacred pipe ceremony was often part of the other traditional ceremonies. The pipe was shared at the appearance of White Buffalo Calf Woman and has been the way to pray, especially for peace and for broken relationships.

Keeping of the soul, *Wanage Yuahapi*, allowed the community to purify the soul of a deceased member.

Hanblecha, or vision quest, was also brought by White Buffalo Calf Woman. Bear Butte, near the sacred Black Hills of South Dakota, is a powerful location where the questing individual fasts to cleanse the soul and meet his or her spirit guide.

Many of these ceremonies and special occasions such as graduations, marriage, births, and naming ceremonies were often accompanied by the giveaway. The sponsors of the ceremony would publically give away their precious possessions as a sign of generosity.

The students at Takini School chose the skyhawk as their mascot. Skyhawks are plentiful on the reservation. They circle with the air currents above the ground getting a broad vision of the surroundings. Their symbolism is that of a messenger. They teach us to be observant and be open to the messages life is sending. The skyhawk's screech definitely wakes us up.

The school motto was *Woonspe Okolakkaiye*, meaning "a learning place for the success of all." The ease and creativity of setting forth long-lasting decisions were the direct result of the freedom experienced by the people in their new-found power of governance.

It was such a privilege and challenge to create and implement an entire curriculum structured around Lakota values. Generally accepted ways of public education were put aside, and a new form was instituted with the blessings of state and federal governments.

Textbooks, the grading system of A-F, and the designation of first through twelfth grade levels were all discarded. Using each Lakota value, we identified as outcomes the skills and knowledge needed for every student to be successful both on and off the reservation when leaving high school. We established benchmarks to show progress. The computer made it possible for each of our approximately 350 students to have their individual records of requirements, progress, and accomplishments.

Learning circles were established to facilitate instruction and to help organize student learning based on their levels of expertise. Staff members were designated as coaches to teach within these learning circles. These coaches included not only the professional teaching staff, including resource room teachers, special education and gifted teachers, and administration, but also the cooks, bus drivers, and janitors. Since these coaches were not educated or prepared for this integrated approach to education, we held staff development and team planning sessions every Friday for two years. The students attended four long days, Monday through Thursday.

What helped make this approach successful? Instead of textbooks and student goals set by an outside entity, the staff designed appropriate thematic units that encompassed the usual disciplines of language arts, math, science, social studies, and the fine arts.

Of course, we were still required to meet state and federal requirements regardless of how we accomplished them. As an example, a thematic unit about astronomy used local traditions of harvesting, hunting, and moving with the seasons on the prairie. Since our school embodied local Lakota traditions, singing and dancing were an integral part of our day. Units were created around preparing the dance outfits, drum building, dancing and singing practices, and Lakota language and ceremony.

A dynamic unit involved building a rodeo arena and powwow, *wacipi*, grounds on-site. Students bought and raised young steers and leased the lighted arena to local ranchers for calf roping using these steers. The state high school rodeo finals were held at our school.

The spiritual path of the Lakota people was deeply imbedded in daily school life. Takini School had its own spiritual leader along with several other holy men who came to pray at school events. Each day began with the flag song honoring those military people who defended our country. The flag song was led by the student drummers and singers. Next, staff and students were individually smudged by a coach upon entering a classroom in a ritual, asking for clearing and blessings.

The school had an on-site sweat lodge as well as our own buffalo herd. Students, staff, and community members had the opportunity to be immersed in tradition. The richness of our days and nights was immeasurable.

The communities united behind the school. The students flourished. The program received national recognition. The opportunities and monies multiplied as we proved to be accountable and successful. Ken and I had originally intended to stay for three years. Instead we stayed for nine years!

These years were an affirmation of what can be accomplished in such a unique arena when one lives within the laws of grace. An abundance of commitment, creativity, and support gave life to a complex educational system.

The divine or the power of love was manifested daily in a most powerful sense as we experienced the dimensionality inherent in traditional ceremony and the joy of singing and dancing. A radiance and clarity permeated our school life alongside the reality of extreme poverty and alcoholism that was so prominent in reservation life. It was like simultaneously participating in parallel universes. Yet we were able to remain healthy and optimistic.

Then it was time to leave. We knew our invitation had run out. We had been invited guests, and now we were no longer needed. It is a gift to recognize endings and to be able to exit quietly. We had accomplished much, had saved money, were healthy, and the new world with all the freedom we would need was ours to embrace. Once again, most of our earthly belongings could fit in our car! We drove off the Cheyenne River Sioux Indian Reservation for the third time, returning to Spearfish.

We had helped our son David purchase a home in Spearfish where he lived with two other young men and three dogs. Since we were coming back, he asked us to live with him after disbursing the roommates and two of the three dogs. Together we totally remodeled the 1907 home, and then welcomed Cori, the love of David's life, to our household. To live with and work alongside of one's grown son is a joy, and we experienced daily an outpouring of pure love and appreciation. We shared this living space for several years with ease.

At that time, our daughter Sharon lived in Phoenix. Just as my parents had loaned us the money to buy our land and to build our home in Spearfish, we helped Sharon buy her home. For a few years we would live with her during the winter, and we moved between homes, without the responsibility of a home of our own.

A renewed connection to Sedona grew stronger, as we would house-sit, dog-sit, and, yes, even chicken-sit, for friends in Sedona during some of the wintermonths. We were living a vagabond existence of abundance and joy, reaping great love from our children and beauty from our surroundings. Even with that, a sense of longing for a home base with a consistent center crept into my consciousness. For twelve years we had been on the move—the reservation, Spearfish, Sedona, and Phoenix. I knew with clarity that change was coming. We trusted that we would be receptive to our next adventure and stage of life.

This refining and questioning stage of life exited on the wings of fire. A week before my sixtieth birthday, I experienced a sudden onset of severe pain beginning at my waist and burning throughout both legs. At first I suspected flu. But I applied my self-regulation and pain management skills to no avail. We even rented a hotel room with a hot tub for relief that didn't happen. After three days I could no longer tolerate the pain and knew it was not the flu. I asked out loud, "What is this?" I clearly heard, "Circulation." I did not question the authenticity of this dimensional Grace-filled experience. I asked, and I received. Immediately my nursing mind came up with, "abdominal aortic aneurism."

I called a local clinic in Spearfish and secured an appointment with a doctor of osteopathy. He had an opening that afternoon. The nurse drew blood, and the doctor performed a cursory physical examination and made an appointment for an electromyogram to rule out spinal stenosis. That test was unremarkable.

But when I called the doctor with the electromyogram test results, he said, "Come in right now. Your sedimentation rate from the blood work is sky-high." The diagnosis was "polymyalgia rheumatica" which is inflammation of the lining of the blood vessels. He told me it was a rare disease with no known cause and no known cure, and that I needed to be on a high dosage of prednisone. The doctor was concerned and made an appointment for me with a rheumatoid specialist in Phoenix, where we were headed for the winter. Naturally, I searched the Internet for information. I rebelled against taking prednisone for more than a few days because of its side effects. However, it truly is a powerful drug. Since the inflammation and pain were greatly reduced within two days, I discontinued it after six days.

The specialist in Phoenix confirmed the diagnosis of PMR and said that I must remain on the prednisone. I asked, "Why?" He said, "You could have a stroke or go blind, or both could occur, as the disease affects the blood vessels in your head." I knew these vessels were affected because I had experienced severe headaches. So I bargained for the lowest effective dosage and asked at what sedimentation rate

I could begin reducing the dosage. The sedimentation rate blood test measures how quickly red blood cells settle in a test tube in one hour. The normal for women is between 0 and 20. Mine was 112. The doctor said when the rate was at 27 I could start tapering off the prednisone. That gave me a clear goal to create a mental and physical healing regimen. I gave thanks for a correct and speedy diagnosis.

Since I had recognized from the beginning that this health challenge was not just about the physical, I asked for guidance and clarity of its meaning in my life at this particular time. Listening for an answer, I heard, "Get a reading from Monitor." I had met the research specialist who channels the Monitor group several years earlier. This was the researcher that had given me suggestions for structuring a research model for the self-regulation program I established in the public school system.

I had come to know that Monitor represents a group of entities not in human form and from another dimension who speaks through my friend when asked. The Monitor group is dedicated to asking us to recognize the divine beings we are. The messages from Monitor challenge and inspire my beliefs and my potential.

I had no idea if personal readings were available, but I had asked for guidance and received an answer. There was no option for me but to follow through. My researcher friend's address was available to me from an earlier conference we had both attended. So I contacted him and had a channeled life reading from Monitor.

All this was a first for me and reinforced my knowing of my spiritual path. Besides providing insight into my life purposes and evolution, Monitor offered me many specific instructions to remediate the PMR and to become healthy and whole once again. These instructions included applying castor oil packs to my abdomen and alkalizing packs over my spleen, as well as continuing the prednisone as directed.

Within seven months from the onset I reached the sedimentation rate negotiated with the doctor and began tapering off the drug dosage. In fourteen months, I was completely healthy. The only lasting side effect? I had gained ten pounds! Although PMR is considered a chronic condition, I know it was a one-time occurrence, as I met the challenge with all my being within the laws of grace.

My sense of grace, my spiritual purpose, and my appreciation of the interconnectedness of all life and all universes greatly expanded at this juncture of my life. I continue to attend monthly gatherings of the Monitor Group. These gatherings are dedicated to their teachings, which have deepened and broadened the beliefs I share here regarding the role of the laws of grace within our earthly lives.

CHAPTER 8

• •

Sharing and Releasing

Age Sixty-One and Onward

*W*e *now had no primary* home, or any home for that matter. Our adult children and our grandchildren were living in South Dakota, Colorado, Arizona, and Virginia. We were free to move between the homes of our children. Our son Michael and his wife Dorothy even said they would create a suite for us in their Virginia home if we would come live with them permanently. Similar invitations were forthcoming from each of our children. We were wholeheartedly welcomed.

We were truly living a daily existence within the laws of grace as evidenced by the expressions of grace. Ken and I had an abundance of resources that provided a base to move among our families for several years. We had saved money while working on the reservation. We were mentally and physically healthy, receptive to the outpouring of love from our families, and grateful for the experience.

I believe in the possibility of a peaceful, joyful existence for every being within our universe. I know it begins with me. It is my birthright to align with grace and live in harmony and beauty. After all, I am created with pure love, and divinity resides in my core. I do not know why, but I have been aware of these laws of grace in this lifetime. Love, trust and beauty swirl around me effortlessly. I recognize this and am profoundly grateful.

This abundance makes it possible to be receptive and to experience the divinity and the power of love with our immediate and extended families. There are minimal expectations, manipulations, or guilt involved in daily or overall interactions. Our family members do not have to consider in their decision-making what I want or expect of them in the big picture. That freedom of expression, knowing that pure love underpins all decisions, does lead to creative receptivity and trust in living our daily lives. We are supported, not judged or punished. I know this is so, as I experienced it, especially sharing family space in this most intimate way. Living in harmony is not just an ideal. It is real.

I did experience physical tiredness during our sojourns with family. In fact, I once made the remark to our son Michael, "I can't live here full time as it's too much work!" My heart would ache whenever I witnessed the pain and frustration within our growing families. I realized living with our children and grandchildren left me open to the emotional impact of their challenges, even though at a deeper level I knew all was in order.

The safer, more comfortable action would be to distance myself by taking a stance of "ignorance is bliss." I did not choose this stance, recognizing I could share with family by holding a space of love and invoking the golden light of grace. My goal was to offer advice only when asked. It continues to be a worthy goal. However, I don't always achieve it!

Though we did not fully realize it at the time, the stage was set for our next life change. We had a house-sitting opportunity in Sedona during one of the winter visits to our daughter Sharon's home in Phoenix. My dear Sedona friend Marlene said, "Loretta, get your real estate license, move to Sedona, and we can share a business." Because I had time during that visit, I attended the ninety hours of instruction, passed the state requirements, and became a licensed real estate agent. It was inspiring to realize I still had the mental and physical prowess to learn a new vernacular and begin another career.

During that same winter visit, I vividly recall making the statement to Ken, "I want to live in Sedona and in a 'Homes by Monty' house." Monty builds custom, Old World homes using his gifts of artistry and intuition. He is conscious of how a home sits on the land, how to frame the views, and respects the dance among materials used, existing vegetation, and the codes that govern home building. It is my knowing that by proclaiming my intention with this statement, I consciously engaged the third law of grace and initiated that manifestation.

Two years later, during our family reunion in Spearfish, South Dakota, my Sedona friend called and said, "Come now; I am opening my own real estate company." My Ken said, "If you want to work again and live in Sedona, I will move with you. You know my role in this lifetime is to support you." Without hesitation I told him, "Yes, this is what I want to do." Ken was not ready to move for several months, so I moved ahead with my plans. I immediately called two different Sedona friends about rental possibilities. The first knew of no rentals. The second friend said, "How synchronistic! The renter of our studio apartment has bought a home and is moving within the week. The apartment is yours if you want it." My answer was yes. I was once again in awe of living within the laws of grace.

Within three days, I had packed my car with what I needed for living in Sedona. Our family reunion was at an end, and our daughter, Sharon, from Phoenix, who had attended the reunion, lovingly forfeited her airplane ticket and drove with me cross-country to Sedona. Within the week I was a real estate agent in Sedona and was settled into a four-hundred-square-foot lower-level studio belonging to our special Sedona friends. This move was accomplished quickly, with ease and with the clarity of living in the flow of what I was creating for our next life adventure.

Sharon provided a love seat and dinette set for the apartment and our friends upstairs provided a bed, dresser, and media cabinet. A sink and refrigerator were already there for us. We bought a hot plate and a used outdoor grill. A bathroom and closet were carved out of this living space.

This was truly simplified living. We had many laughs at our living situation. If I misplaced something, I could stand in the center of the room and rotate in a circle to find it. One night I had gone to bed, and Ken was watching television about five feet away. I asked him to please turn down the volume. He responded, "What's your problem? I'm out here in the living room!" With humor and love, we successfully honored each other's requests.

Our daily life was simple, filled with love and the beauty of desert living. Javelinas, tarantulas, and coyotes roamed across our driveway. Rattlesnakes, scorpions, and rabbits were also visitors in this rural village a few miles from Sedona. The environment demanded alertness and an appreciation for diversity. Although I was driving daily throughout red-rock country in my role as real estate agent, this home base, with our spiritual friends living above us, was nourishing for body and soul.

This "temporary" home lasted four years. I have no doubt that living in our tiny studio rental for this length of time was the result of the intention set into motion when I declared, "I want to live in Sedona and in a 'Homes by Monty' house." As a real estate agent, I was constantly alerted to possible houses or land for our next home. I trusted it would manifest, and I let go of timelines for this to happen.

Land did become available in my most attractive area of this red-rock country. Monty agreed to build us a home at an unbelievably low price that we could afford. In return, we helped him buy land where he could build speculative homes to sell. Our arrangement included the stipulation that we had no input in the building process or in establishing timelines. This accounts for the years in our studio rental. The arrangement was tenable as we trusted Monty to build us a home of beauty and harmony, and we knew it would be built on our sacred spot.

This story is a concrete example of how powerfully we are living within the laws of grace. This home supports such joy in our lives. We acknowledge and are grateful each day for our sanctuary. We do not have to earn such favor. It is our birthright. We live in respect and love, and surrender to the power of that love.

As I view the next stage of my life, I realize that the earlier years we spent in Sedona pursuing our family health-centered resort dream had prepared me in unexpected ways. During those years I bought and had operated a home health care business with the help of a friend. My conscious reason for this endeavor was for financial support as I explored Sedona. My business partner and I interviewed individuals who needed care to remain in their homes. We then provided and monitored care providers who worked with us to aid those clients.

Looking back, the eighteen months operating this home health care business had provided an opportunity to truly recognize and express the result of grace in my life. I had been open and receptive to buying this homespun business that was run out of a van, a business that community leaders said wasn't a sound investment. I possessed enough medical knowledge to safely interpret custodial care needs of people wanting to remain in their homes. I knew I could trust in abundance if I had altruistic intentions in running this business.

My partner and I continually remarked on our ability to know and then confirm between ourselves if a particular caretaker who applied was right for us to place with clients. We knew that dimensionality of knowing was grace at work, and we never doubted our decisions. We accurately placed the appropriate caregivers with the right clients. Even more outstanding was the fact that a balance was maintained between those needing and those giving care. It was not always an easy ride, since we were on call twenty-four hours, seven days a week. Lots of last-minute scrambling, and the need to stay calm and positive to maintain harmony, was required in the home health care business.

We had contact with clients who were essentially the pioneers who had settled this region. Serving clients throughout the whole region offered me a running start in the real estate business. I had come to know the layout of the area and, more importantly, the deep stories and the heartbeat of the land.

This sojourn several years ago had helped set the stage for this later time in my life. This time I refer to as "sharing and releasing." Sedona is my home for now, and real estate is my everyday activity that keeps me connected to community and demands continual creative action.

The invitation by my dear Sedona friend to share in the dream of owning her own real estate company and sharing the workload is now a fully realized manifestation. It is a joy to be part of a company with heart that functions as family without the usual pressure to perform. Presently we are co-owners of our company and are working as one.

Being a business owner again was not planned or consciously desired. Yet I was receptive to the possibility and was willing to invest our savings in order to continue doing real estate with freedom and the clarity of intent set forth in our company goals.

The real estate business is a challenging and rewarding avenue for me to share a lifetime of experience. It seems intense vignettes or individual stories are played out as people buy and sell their homes or land. I am chosen to direct the process for their highest needs, bring closure to the scene and move on, or release that portion of their lives.

At this stage of life, I am mature and wise enough not to become attached to the drama that often accompanies real estate transactions. I can observe, problem-solve, support the process, and keep the final outcome in view as people find or release their sanctuary or albatross.

Some real estate transactions have resulted in adding beautiful, heartfelt friends to my life. What began as a need focused on real estate has turned into deeply shared interactions of joy, trust, and love. Of course, my deeply held relationships have also led to real estate transactions as a byproduct of that trust and love. I experience an intertwining of personal and professional lives with minimum delineation or compartmentalization. They stream together, giving me a path to be of service and to be served. It is a powerful avenue or opening for me to share love, joy, and beauty at this particular junction of life.

A second quality prominent during this chapter of grace present in my life is that of release. Release is a dynamic present throughout my life and is especially potent in my seventieth decade. I released each of our five offspring from our home and protection out into the wider world to live their individual lives. In fact, it seems to be continuous release each time we physically come together and then separate.

In our early adult years, we were continually on the move from state to state and home to home. With each move, we let go of our stuff, our home, the proximity of friends, and our jobs and daily routines. This was physically tiring, yet the chaos, or shaking up of the status quo, and excitement brought about by the unknown and possibilities always outshone the sadness of letting go. We trusted in abundance and in the sense that even more joy and opportunity lay ahead. And with each move, it did.

I had continued to collect educational degrees, certifications, and professional experiences. It seemed I was regularly preparing, poised and receptive to opportunities to manifest the divine. I know one reason this attitude and lifestyle was possible is that I wholeheartedly experienced and continue to experience pure love from Ken and our children.

As time passed, locations changed, and my work in the world changed, I released and let lapse my teaching certificate and my affiliation with national professional organizations—the American Holistic Health Society, the Institute of Noetic Sciences, and the Biofeedback Society of America. I most recently canceled my first professional designation—my certification as a registered nurse. Each time I allowed a certification or license to expire, a certain identity and responsibility I had earlier assumed was lifted. My ties with many people were released, and I was well aware I was letting go of much more than a certificate. Freedom and loss were equally experienced and appreciated, mostly for the new space that opened up.

I have come to know that relationships are more important to me than material articles, and they require more effort to release. Both my mother and my father were grand teachers for me as they approached their physical deaths.

My father quietly endured chemotherapy when he was diagnosed with Hodgkin's lymphoma at the age of seventy-two. He and my mother formed their own supportive unit, yet always counted on me to advocate for their medical needs. Even on my father's deathbed, he joyfully opened his arms to all his family around his bed and said, "This is what it is all about!"

My releasing of father came when I rehearsed out loud and with flowing tears the words I would say to him, giving him my permission to leave and assuring him we were all going to be okay. I actually said the words to him with relative ease and strength. Father reciprocated with a smile and a loving embrace. My mother accepted his imminent passing with a peaceful attitude that enveloped us all. She did regret for a moment that she was not present with him at the exact time of his passing. Yet, perhaps that was his plan. I believe we each choose the immediate circumstances of our passing.

My mother's passing seemed initially full of drama and then peaceful. For two years after father's passing, she fared well. Mother assumed the existence of a widow without angst and self-pity. She went out to eat by herself, maintained the acres of land on which she lived, and relished time with her extended family as we were all within minutes of her farm.

That extended family included my brother, whose wife asked him for a divorce after twenty-four years of marriage. He was despondent and relied on Mother for comfort. Mother told me one day that she could handle such pain when father was alive but not by herself. Her intestines had literally become tied in knots.

One day, in agonizing pain, Mother admitted herself to the local hospital. She had an obstructed bowel, and the doctors recommended immediate surgery. Mother insisted on waiting for me until I returned that evening from an educational consultation on the Pine Ridge Indian Reservation. The surgical team awaited the outcome of our conversation. I explained to mother that death from a ruptured bowel could be most painful. Mother decided to have surgery that night, and the obstruction was removed.

The surgeon then told Mother that minute cancer cells were scattered throughout her abdomen, and he wanted to do chemotherapy immediately. Mother said no. The doctor was angry with her for not accepting his treatment. Mother was not to be coerced and stuck to her decision, realizing she had my full support and my brother's support as well. The doctor then said that no further care besides the usual postoperative procedures would be offered her. Because the insurance coverage allowed for surgery recovery was limited, Mother was to be discharged from the hospital within the week. However, she would need twenty-four hour care until tubes were removed.

My brother was still teaching school for another two weeks. I was still closing up my private practice as a psychotherapist to devote full time to her care. We needed more time. I negotiated with the hospital administrator to allow her to remain in the hospital and pay half of the going room rates. As a businessman, the administrator knew some income was better than an empty room. My nursing background gave me the knowledge and courage to stand up to the system. My mother merited the dignity of having a choice as to how the last months of her earthly life would play out.

When all was in place, Mother was moved to her home. She was joyful, especially since she had thought she would not be able to return home. Unknown to me, the hospital staff had been making nursing home plans, and Mother had overheard their conversations.

Mother had underestimated the outpouring of pure love that was hers to claim. She was receptive to our love and care with profound gratitude and dignity.

Mother's surgical wounds healed within six weeks. She did not resume eating and was looking forward to passing. On many occasions she would experience through dimensions the presence of Father. These interactions were as real as lying in her bed and visiting with family.

Over the next three months, she methodically finished up her earthly work. The most difficult was calling in my brother's ex-wife and coming to peace with the divorce. I was continually amazed at what I observed. For the most part I remained detached from her process during our intense last months together.

Mother would ask me to recite the rosary with her as I had done as a youngster. When she came to the phrase in the "Our Father" prayer, "as we forgive those who trespass against us," she could not say it out loud. Mother knew, as did I, that she would have conversations and then release her judgments and pain involving particular circumstances. Visiting with her former daughter-in-law was an example of such a release.

During these three months we were bathed in the golden light of grace with so much love and gratitude present. Mother was fully conscious, not medicated, simply waiting to pass. At night, she regularly said to my brother or to me, "Good-bye. And if I'm still here in the morning, it's good night!"

The intensity of the care she needed and the abandonment of most other aspects of daily life was not always easy and without strife. However, my brother and I knew that we were privileged to attend and witness our mother's transition. My love and respect for my brother grew as he assumed equal care of our dying mother. Often this care is the province of women, and men stand back. This was not so with him. Some friends and acquaintances would say, "I bet it will be a relief for everyone when your mother goes." I came to realize they did not know the depth of joy that we were experiencing. I would experience a radiance emanating around her and feel bathed in a field of pure love. Mother allowed me to partake in her trust and clarity of the potential of life beyond this earthly life.

Mother asked that she be buried in her wedding dress. She offered no explanation. Of course her wish was fulfilled. I knew that Mother had desired the contemplative life when she was young. I believe she knew that she soon would truly be the "bride of Christ."

All was in order, and on a July Sunday at noon, mother's face transfigured briefly into the image of Jesus Christ. Up until that moment, Mother had been alert, sitting up in her bed, and nothing seemed different in outward appearances. With that transfiguration, she drew her last quiet breaths and was gone. Mother died with the beauty and dignity with which she lived.

Mother's passing left an immediate void in our daily life. Yet we experienced a sense of surrender and joy that she had experienced a peaceful transition and was free. My brother remarked, "We are orphans again." This was a reference to those days following our births when we were abandoned by birth parents and had not yet been placed with our lifetime parents. It was surprising to have those thoughts and emotions arise. Yet it seems we recognized them and then released them.

As I was contemplating writing this chapter, I first titled it, "Share, Release, and Rest." I found no stores of rest coming forth that were not contrived. I know, for me at this time, one meaning of rest is "The rest …"

"The rest ..." is a big unknown, and I feel wide open to manifest the divine through grace. My family, my home, my friends, and my work are presently interacting in radiant harmony. I truly have no inkling of what will be next. Nor do I have any future intention formed at the present moment. It feels as if I am supported in a sea of potential and know that all is within the field of grace and its natural organization. I have no doubt that the next adventure will be forthcoming. For now, the peace and joy of just floating is enough and is appreciated.

I am wondering if my life pattern of making waves in the calm sea of peace and joy will once again create motion or whitecaps that reveal my next passion and project. My friend, Jeannie, describes it as "stirring the pot" and recognizing what comes to the top as a signal for action. That act of making waves, or stirring the pot, reveals the focus of creating and then fulfilling a vision that brings the bliss I have come to expect. Right now, in my seventh decade, it is an exciting challenge to imagine having the tenacity and vision to create anew. I am staying tuned.

CHAPTER 9

● ● ● ● ● ● ● ● ● ● ● ● ● ● ● ● ●

Becoming an Agent of Grace

As an individual agent of grace, I am evolving and coming to know my authenticity. By authenticity, I mean coming to know I am a radiant and an infinite being not bound by culture, dogma, and worldly rules that define and confine who I am. I know I am a unique person with unique gifts. I truly trust the impulses and the calls to action that sound from deep within myself. And because I trust, there is no doubt that I care deeply for myself and the world, and I step forward to make a difference.

I recall my experiences as a health professional and an educator. In my early thirties, before wellness was an accepted concept, I knew to focus my efforts on creating health and not on solving problems. Even though I had been educated in the medical and educational fields, where the main focus was identifying an area of weakness and remediating the problem, I refused to develop protocols for stress management, stress-related illness, and ineffective behaviors and concerns, such as learning disabilities. Just using these descriptions in the previous sentence sets the focus on problems and the need for treatment. Instead, I felt compelled to use language that described well-being and enhanced performance.

As a teacher in the public schools, I saw my students set goals for positive change such as, "I speak in public feeling confident and at ease," or, "I relax fully between wrestling matches to conserve energy and to refresh my body and mind." I was continually taught by my students when they articulated specific goals in the areas of performance and relationships as reasons for learning self-regulation skills offered within the school curriculum. I acknowledge the impact of having responded to that authentic self's call to insist that this self-regulation program remain in the growth and not the remediation arena.

Let us listen to that authentic level of knowing as we reach into the higher order of grace that supports our call to action—that call to serve, that call to create the future. When we act with authenticity, each thought, word, and action is creating that future now. My Native American friends express this in their seventh generation philosophy, which says the consequences of our thoughts and actions this moment are experienced seven generations from now. How powerful that we are the vehicle through which the creator-of-all is creating the foundation of the future. As agents of grace, we have the responsibility to choose our thoughts and behaviors within the higher organization of grace. As we embrace the acts of grace, we are uplifted and fearless as we envision and enliven our very being in the now. Let us fully embrace the fact that we create the future now. The future depends on us!

One of the ways I am coming to know and be my authentic self is by resting. When I first added the attribute of rest to the title of the last chapter of my life stages, I could not bring forth stories of rest to serve as examples. Thus I removed "Rest" from the title, and it become "Sharing and Releasing—Ages Sixty-One and Onward." However, it soon became clear that I wanted to articulate what rest means to me beyond the rest of my story. I do know that for me, rest is not just a time out for relaxation and rejuvenation.

Rest is residing within the order of grace, recognizing my higher, or soul's, purpose, and trusting the love and wisdom of being authentic to direct my thoughts and actions. I do not have to consider the consequences and "shoulds" of doing what I choose to do. In rest, polarities are collapsed, and I sense that oceanic feeling of oneness. In other words, the bigger picture of how the parts come together to form the whole becomes evident. I have only to be the unique, loving, serving, and radiant being that I am. When I say, "I love you," and approach any situation with love, I am issuing an oath of allegiance to a higher order of being. With that oath, I am committed to living within the flow or order of grace.

I am coming to know what rest looks like. At rest, I am alert and ready to be surprised. There is no expectation, no striving, no goal setting, no need for seeking and questioning. Having no stake in the outcomes, I cannot be traumatized, wounded, or disappointed. At rest, there is awareness, gratitude, acceptance, compassion, and respect for the process of being. When I am truly at rest, I let go of all my need for knowledge and expertise. I shed the persona and identity I have spent a lifetime accumulating. With that surrender of who or what I need to be, comes such relief, such freedom. I am content, at ease, still, and free. I am truly at rest. Lao Tzu says, "When I let go of what I am, I fully become what I might be."

From the position of rest, I can more fully be an agent of grace at the individual level. Observing my daily thoughts and behaviors, I realize I am more awake in noticing events, situations, and attached meanings. I observe their interrelationships and make new meaning, recognizing the seeming paradoxes in some instances. I continually acknowledge the synchronicity within the events, thoughts, and situations. I am coming to know rest.

A meaningful understanding of being an agent of grace at rest came during my experience of flying frequently to our family events. We all experience security practices now in place, which were generated from the fear response following perceived threats to our safety. As I remove my own shoes, jackets, and any metal, and watch my Ken go through an entire pat down each and every time because of his artificial metal hip, I invoke the golden light of grace to surround all persons present, and I invite goodwill and an uplifting journey for all. What a paradox this is—that a procedure generated from fear gives us time to slow our steps, be noticed, and even touched! It is impossible to be invisible. We shed some of our stuff and have a moment of recognition with smiles or nods. Then we pay close attention to gathering what we have put down and head off in the right directions awaiting the next boarding procedure. I can just hear you say, "That's one way of looking at it."

On each flight, I actually am amazed by the community congregated within the body of the plane. We move through the atmosphere as one, trusting as we are carried on wings of love and the expertise that supports flight. As an agent of grace, I consciously look at my companion flyers, expand heart love, and fill the cabin with golden light of grace. Then all there is to do is sit back and appreciate the organization of grace that assures all is in divine order.

I am coming to recognize that at rest, experiences come and go. I notice my environment through my senses. I notice my thoughts and feelings. Yet I am not those sensations, those thoughts, and those feelings. I am pure awareness that includes sensations, thoughts, and feelings.

The position of rest is an important avenue to be an agent of grace. I am discovering I can cooperate with others and be of service when I am alert, and I let go of expectations of others, of myself, and of the idea that I need to do something or that you need to do something. Such freedom and pure love result from being totally present to another person or a situation with the intent of being of service.

How do we become fully present? We acknowledge that the field, the context surrounding an event, is equally as important as the event or what is happening. We bring all our consciousness to the fullness of that moment. In that present moment there is not past or future. It is all present.

Grace is offered here as a channel to pure awareness. Through grace, we can know unity where all is interrelated. Our challenge is to recognize and appreciate those expressions and results of grace present in our daily lives. We are challenged to accept that our altruistic intentions are supported within a higher order, an organizational pattern, available to help us be pure awareness and at rest. Grace is guidance, a channel, offered each of us to know our divinity, to be at rest, recognizing our relationship with the whole, and to be of uplifting service to all creation.

On an individual level, we come to be an agent of grace by steadfastly choosing to live daily life within the organization of grace. We recognize the expressions of grace. We celebrate the results of grace now evident throughout our lives. When experiencing the results of grace, notice the full context, including the background or space in which that clarity, joy, dimensionality, freedom, synchronicity, and radiance are present. Embody that sacred moment in which you acknowledge that you are manifesting the divine and you recognize all is one, or infinity.

May we be aware each moment of our thoughts, feelings, and actions. That awareness, that attention, opens the opportunity for choice. We can notice and choose to release our fears and our expectations, recognizing that if we cooperate, in other words surrender, to the force of love we are calling divinity, we can choose to move within the higher order of grace.

It does take humility to reduce and even release our identity—our image by which we let others know us. Often that identity boxes us in and limits our own perception of our potential. If we are to progress and broaden our capacity to cooperate and serve, we will expand who we think we are and how others accept us. We will not only change but also release the boundaries established for our identity. So often we become locked into a niche by our family and by our culture's expectations of what we should believe and how we should act. We further establish boundaries by educational and career choices and by the roles we have chosen to accept.

By the time I was twenty-seven, my hair had turned white. My hair no longer held color by the time I was thirty-seven. So I was a white-haired woman at thirty-eight years of age. That fact seems truly insignificant, yet I quickly learned the stereotypes associated with white or gray hair. Little ones called me "Grandma" as I entered a classroom. Strangers expected more experience or wisdom than I had yet acquired.

Many new friends, especially on the university campus where I was pursuing a graduate degree, couldn't decide what generation I belonged to! They asked me "How old are you, Loretta? We don't know how we are expected to act around you." I must say I grinned at the confusion and, for the most part, chose how I wanted others, including professors, to identify me. I realized having white hair allowed me to be outside the box of usual expectations. I had freedom to play with my responses to people and situations. I celebrated the insight and flexibility such an insignificant event as having white hair offered me.

My learning was an awareness of how physical characteristics, expectations set forth by cultural interpretations, and my own sense of self-identity set parameters. I can accept, expand, or totally step outside of and reject those parameters.

With such awareness, each of us can say, "I choose to be who I was born to be. I will exemplify love and the expressions of grace as only I can do." No other person can express or be us. Every being is unique. Indeed we have the freedom and responsibility to fully be our unique selves as agents of grace.

In becoming agents of grace, first of all we serve ourselves. We do that by honoring and respecting our bodies and our uniqueness of mind, emotions and spirit. We choose nourishing foods and environments. We choose supportive people with whom to interact. We may choose to withdraw from people and factors that do not add well-being to our daily lives. We continually move toward acceptance and unconditional love of ourselves. Coming from that core of love, we can truly be agents of grace in service of others.

Next, we serve others by gaining and then sharing expertise and experience. During my time as a classroom teacher, I pledged to consider the whole child when preparing a learning opportunity for the students in my care. I prepared the lessons recognizing learning styles and situational interferences, as well as the motivation and capacity of each child.

Jacob was a particular challenge. He had been labeled learning disabled since kindergarten and was now in the seventh grade. Jacob did not connect letters and numbers in the same form and sequence as a majority of the students. He could listen and then learn new information by kinesthetically placing the new information in a special organizational pattern he had developed. This pattern connected the new information with his present knowledge. Although Jacob could not write what he had learned, he could speak or demonstrate the acquisition of the new learning. That was more than good enough for me.

Another student, Jennifer, read the directions and quickly

completed the basic requirements of the lesson. It was up to me as her teacher to coach her to take a further step by applying that new knowledge to her own circumstances and to its potential usefulness in her young life. As a result, after completing one assignment, Jennifer constructed a needs assessment. The assessment determined that a majority of her classmates wanted to know what happened to pets, especially large animals like horses, when they became ill, were injured, or even died. She went on to contact a local veterinarian and set up a time for him to talk to the class and answer questions. Jennifer executed her plan beyond the basic requirements of the lesson assigned.

My biggest challenge was to serve each of the twenty-two students in my care, honoring their uniqueness. The ease with which I often accomplished this delighted me. I always began a class by creating what I called a "sacred space." In that space, we declared we were a unit united by love and respect. Seventh-graders were willing to fully embrace those qualities of belonging to the unit and being recognized for their creativity and risk-taking as they accepted the safety of a loving, supportive environment. I dare say, what group wouldn't thrive if they were celebrated and valued for their contributions to the process at hand?

As agents of grace, we heed the calling. We accept the responsibility to step forth within our families, chosen groups, and our communities to serve, to uplift, to recognize untapped potential, and to celebrate diverse contributions that every individual person and every distinct group offers the larger community. Now is the time to establish and gather in groups as agents of grace. As we do this, we enhance the power and love inherent within the laws of grace multifold. As Aristotle declared, "The whole is greater than the sum of its parts." We come together with intention and purpose acknowledging the need for and the presence of trust and gratitude for the support offered by the group.

A group that I have been part of for ten years offers service where need is perceived. We have remodeled a senior center gathering room, created an inviting living space for abused women and children needing a safe place, offered scholarships for higher education, and completed many more projects. Small contributions of service at the local level uplift the participants and the whole community. Love and goodwill are contagious and are passed forward.

I invite you to acknowledge those groups where you are a member, where they exist for altruistic service. Recognize the beauty, ease, and the abundance of resources and love present as you offer service within the order of grace. With grace, love replaces fear and the sense of lack. With grace, we act with caring, compassion, and patience without considering how it may benefit us.

With a growing understanding and the experience of the power and ease of living within the order of grace, we can choose to become agents of grace. An agent of grace serves. The ways we come to serve are as unique as we are as individuals or groups. I serve because I know that my physical and mental health are enhanced by reaching out and doing. I serve because I am grateful. My friend has been given a second chance at life, having been healed of cancer. She knows she serves by being available with compassion for others facing similar crises and by sharing her experiences. Many serve by intentionally praying for and invoking the golden light of grace for those persons asking for help. We serve by playing, working, and interacting with integrity, conscious of our impact as we live our daily lives.

As agents of grace, we serve self, community, country, and even the planet with pure love and wisdom without expectation of rewards, recognition, or reciprocal action. Of course, as agents of grace, we may receive acknowledgment for our service, but it is not the motivation or expectation for providing the service.

As agents of grace, whether at the individual, group, or planetary level, we find ourselves living within the laws of grace. We know grace expresses divinity, the force of love, and is all pervasive and available to all. We accept that grace is interlaced with love, and our role is to surrender. We experience grace channeling power. Many of our manifestations are the results of that power.

In order to ground this concept of agents of grace, I have shared the experiences and ideas coming into my daily consciousness. I have done this not to exclude your experiences or to set me apart, but to inspire and invite you to identify your stories and knowings. Your own particular experiences and ideas will assist you in exploring the beauty, challenge, and love in every moment, and help you recognize the presence and power of grace in your life.

With grace, we step off the wheel of karma. Grace does not negate the wheel of karma. We transcend it. We can always step back on the wheel and live within the law of karma. When I speak of the law of karma, I simply mean cause and effect. My selfish actions bring a reaction. This is often expressed as, "What goes around, comes around." Within this context, the law of karma takes effect when we act with selfish intentions. For example, we may join a group out of fear of being alone or not belonging. We are under the illusion we are separate. We want to be reassured we have value, we are acceptable, and we are loved. That fearful, selfish position could easily lead to the result of our expectations of the group not being met. Thus continues the cycle of feeling rejected and of not belonging. The wheel of karma brings lessons. We keep circling until we develop the awareness we are divine. We are love.

We can be liberated by choosing to live within the laws of grace.

The infallible way to be within the organization of grace is to be aware of others and respond graciously to their needs. The order of grace invites all to the experience of oneness, where form and spirit are united. Grace is our birthright. Let us invoke grace for ourselves, our community, and our planet. Now is the time.

BIBLIOGRAPHY

Balsekar, Ramesh S. *The End of Duality.* Mumbai, India: Yogi Impressions, Thomson Press, 2009.

Black Elk, Wallace and William Lyon. *Black Elk: The Sacred Ways of a Lakota.* San Francisco: Harper Collins, 1991.

Butcher, Carmen A. *The Cloud of Unknowing.* Boston and London: Shambhala, 2009.

Dinesen, Isak. *Anecdotes of Destiny and Ehrengard.* Includes the short story "Babette's Feast." New York: Vintage International, 1993.

Dyer, Wayne W. *The Secrets to Manifesting Your Destiny.* Niles, IL: Nightingale Conant CD, 1999.

Fehmi, Les and George Fritz. *The Open Focus Handbook.* Princeton, NJ: Biofeedback Computers, 1982

Felini, Federico and Roberto Rossellini. *The Flowers of St. Frances.* (1950).

Gandhi, Mohandas Karamchand. *An Autobiography: The Story of My Experiments With Truth.* New York: Dover, 1940.

Grady, Harvey and Julie. *Explore with Monitor: Lessons for Freeing Yourself.* Bloomington, IN: iUniverse, 2008.

Klieger, Jackie. Cover photograph, jklieg@aol.com, 2013.

Langham, Derald G. *Genesa: An Attempt to Develop a Conceptual Model to Synthesize, Synchronize, and Vitalize Man's Interpretation of Universal Phenomena.* Fallbrook, CA: Aero, 1969.

Mails, Thomas E. *Fools Crow Wisdom and Power.* Tulsa, OK: Council Oak Books, 1991.

Myss, Carolyn. Channeling Grace: invoking the power of the divine. Boulder, CO: Sounds True CD, 2008.

Porette, Margaret. *The Mirror of Simple Souls.* Notre Dame, IN: Notre Dame Press, 1999.

Sams, Jamie. *Sacred Path Cards.* Harper Collins, 1990.

Spretnak, Charlene. *States of Grace, the Recovery of Meaning in the Postmodern Age.* San Francisco: Harper San Francisco, 1993.

Swanson, Claude. *The Synchronized Universe: New Science of the Paranormal.* Tucson, AZ: Poseidia Press, 2003.

Swimmer, Brian. "The Powers of the Universe." *EnlightenNEXT,* 47, (2011).

Tolle. Eckhart. *A New Earth, Awakening to Your Life's Purpose.* New York: Penguin Group, Plume Printing, 2006.

Wilber, Ken. *No Boundary: Eastern and Western Approaches to Personal Growth.* Boulder, CO: Shambhala, 1979.

Woods, Ted and Wambli Afraid of Hawk. *A Boy Becomes a Man at Wounded Knee.* New York: Walker, 1992.

Witt, Janise. Author photograph. Photographybyjanise.com, 2013.